The Second Time Around

Renewal after age 70,
an astrological perspective

Written, edited and researched by
Joyce & Barry Hopewell

HopeWell
Knutsford, England

First published in English in 2023 by HopeWell

HopeWell, 130 Grove Park, Knutsford,
Cheshire WA16 8QD, UK

Copyright © 2023 HopeWell.

This is an original work by the authors, and no AI was used at any stage. All rights reserved. No part of this publication may be reproduced, sorted in a retrieval system, or transmitted in any form or by any means, electronic or otherwise, without prior permission of the publisher.

Jacket: design by Barry Hopewell,
lotus image by Marc Andreu, licensed via Shutterstock

Horoscopes: Huber Method
(drawn up with MegaStar software)

ISBN: 978-0-9956736-7-0

"We shall not cease from exploration
And the end of all our exploring
Will be to arrive where we started
And know the place for the first time."

T.S.Eliot, Little Gidding

"The only wisdom we can hope to acquire
Is the wisdom of humility; humility is endless"

T.S.Eliot, East Coker

About the Authors

After obtaining her Diploma in Astrological Psychology, Joyce Hopewell became Principal of the English Huber School in 1991. She continued to play a leading role as Principal, then Principal Emeritus, until the closure of the School's teaching programme at the end of 2019.

Barry Hopewell has been chief editor of the publisher HopeWell since its founding in 2003, publisher of the Huber books in English. Also played various roles in the Astrological Psychology Association from 2003 until the organisation's formal closure in 2021.

Acknowledgements

We have drawn upon the wisdom of many researchers and practitioners mentioned in the bibliography and are grateful to all of them for showing the possibilities and challenges of this later stage of life.

This book would also not be possible without the inputs received from the recipients of our survey, in the English- and German-speaking areas, as laid out in the stories in Chapter 5.

Special thanks are due to Harald Zittlau for soliciting inputs in the German-speaking Huber family on our behalf, and to Sue Lewis and John Grove for their additional contributions, and to those non-astrological friends and family who tolerated our requests for input.

Contents

Chapter 1. Introduction 1

Chapter 2. What the Hubers said about The Second Time Around. 5

Chapter 3. What other authors say about this stage of life. 21

Chapter 4. Our survey 31

Chapter 5. Selected stories. 35

5.1 Stories from the 12th House 35

5.2 Stories from the 1st House 90

5.3 Stories from the 2nd and 3rd Houses 135

Chapter 6. Conclusion 157

Appendix 1. Write your own Life Review 165

Appendix 2. Survey guidelines as sent out. 173

Bibliography 179

Chapter 1. Introduction

Bruno Huber's Age Progression

Bruno Huber was a researcher and innovator in astrology, psychology and the relationship between the two. In 1959-1961 Bruno and his wife and fellow seeker Louise were invited by Roberto Assagioli to his Institute of Psychosynthesis in Florence. Bruno helped Assagioli with documenting his system of psychosynthesis and Assagioli mentored Bruno in his astrological-psychological researches, making available his patients and the extensive patient records at the Institute. From this collaboration the system of Huber Astrology, or Astrological Psychology, eventually emerged. The story is told in the Hubers' biography[1].

One of the major innovations that emerged as part of the Hubers' system was Age Progression, whereby the various astrological features in a birth chart are highlighted at particular stages of life, as the Age Point travels around the birth chart. Age Progression is extensively documented in their book *Life Clock*[2], and has proved an invaluable tool for astrological psychologists over many years.

The journey around the Life Clock begins at the Ascendant (AC) of the birth chart, and the Age Point takes 72 years to go around the Clock. At age 70-72 the cycle begins again, signalling another phase of life. What is this phase about, and how does it relate to earlier life? There appears to be much less

---

[1] Hopewell, Barry & Joyce, *Piercing the Eggshell*, HopeWell, 2022
[2] Huber, Bruno & Louise, *Life Clock*, HopeWell, 2006, 2022

known about this, maybe because, on entering this phase, many practitioners of astrological psychology no longer have the motivation to put stuff out 'in the world'.

Why we wrote The Second Time Around

The idea for this book came into being at the end of a meal at our kitchen table. We were probably finishing a last glass of wine and talking generally about life, ours in particular, which was beset with events we were trying to make sense of.

We'd recently been propelled back to an episode in our lives some 36 to 40 years previously, at a time when our Age Points had been in the 7th house, at one end of the Encounter Axis in the natal chart. We were looking back and reflecting on this period of life from the position of being once again, by Age Point, in the 1st house and opposite the 7th at the other end of the Encounter Axis.

From the perspective of the 1st house, we were aware of how different we both were now from the people we'd been 36 years previously, particularly in the context of friendships and relationships. Reconnection with a friendship from that time had recently turned unpleasantly sour and bitter and had ended. We were working through the aftereffects of this experience and recognised that we were seeing it – from our current viewpoint of the 1st house – in a new light. Personal insights came thick and fast. Some demanded attention; being in the 1st house for the second time gave us the opportunity to start afresh, clear the residue of the past and move forward.

We reflected on the fact that, although the theory of the second time around the Life Clock, from around age 70, was well documented by the Hubers, there was little practical experience documented. It seemed that astrological psychologists perhaps lost interest around this stage of their lives; perhaps they had moved on.

"Why don't we do some research and write a book?" The question emerged from the conversation and was immediately dismissed, only to re-emerge later. "The Second Time Around" would not go away, so we contacted others in the same age group to see if there was any shared similarity of experiencing moving forward into this new stage of life, of resolving things from the past and embracing a kind of rebirth.

This book

This book is the story of these people's experiences at this stage of life, together with our tentative conclusions on what we can learn from this.

In the process we try to answer questions. What did the Hubers say about this phase of life? What do other authors say about it? Can we find evidence of the validity of the Hubers' theories for this stage of life?

To this end, we describe a survey we performed, and its results. From this, we have extracted stories which demonstrate Age Progression in action in this later stage of life, using the real life experiences of those who responded.

We hope this might stimulate others to do further research, and particularly with their own birth chart. In particular, we observe that Age Progression provides a valuable tool to help with any process of Life Review, which has been suggested to be a valuable part of the aging process in the later stages of life[3].

It is clear that, at this stage of life, we each have a choice. "The Second Time Around" can mean doing the same thing over again, repeating something, going back to what is familiar, or giving something or someone a second chance. In the context of Age Progression, where we grow older and hopefully wiser, it's more of an opportunity to move on to a higher turn of the spiral and renew and refresh our lives.

Is it just for astrologers?

The content of this book is essentially about the house system and Age Progression, with other astrological features referred to by individual respondents. Perhaps surprisingly, the essence of Age Progression is easily understood by non-astrologers. The progression of the Age Point through the houses in 6-year stages and the echoes that can occur in life every 36 years do not require significant astrological knowledge, and some of our respondents are non-astrologers.

However, to get the most from this book you will need to understand a bit about astrological psychology. There is a good introduction to the subject in Joyce's book *The Cosmic Egg Timer*[4] and detailed coverage of Age Progression in her book *Using Age Progression*[5].

---

[3] On Life Review, see e..g. Robinson, John C, *The Three Secrets of Aging: A Radical Guide*, O-Books, 2012
[4] Hopewell, Joyce and Llewellyn, Richard, *The Cosmic Egg Timer: Introducing Astrological Psychology*, HopeWell 2004, 2011, 2018.
[5] Hopewell, Joyce, *Using Age Progression: Understanding Life's Journey*, HopeWell 2013.

Chapter 2. What the Hubers said about The Second Time Around.

Age Progression. A quick summary.

First, we summarise some of the basics of the Hubers' method of Age Progression, which is comprehensively described in the book *Life Clock*[6].

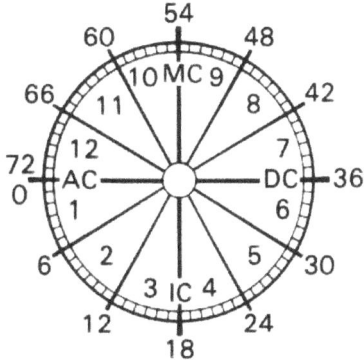

Figure 1 The Life Clock

The Huber birth chart contains 12 houses, numbered 1-12, starting from the Ascendant (AC) and counting up anticlockwise around the chart[7].

In Age Progression, the Age Point (AP) starts at the Ascendant (AC) at birth and progresses anticlockwise around the houses, 6 years to each house. It thus takes 12x6=72 years to complete the cycle around the clock. At age 72 the AP begins the journey around the houses for the second time.

---

[6] Huber, Bruno & Louise, *Life Clock*, HopeWell 2006, 2022.
[7] Huber, Bruno & Louise, *The Astrological Houses*, HopeWell 2011.

Each house corresponds to a distinctive psychological phase of life, roughly categorised as:

1. Formation of the 'I', the ego
2. Creation of personal life, awareness of possessions
3. Learning and education
4. Moving away from the parental home
5. Experiment with and testing life experience
6. Coping with and establishing existence
7. Outward focus – relationships and partnerships
8. Midlife crisis; transformation, change, rebirth
9. Formation of personal life philosophy
10. Self-realisation, authority, individuation
11. Freely chosen relationships, like-minded people
12. Introversion, withdrawal, solitude, facing old age

The process of psychological change from one house to the next begins around the time when the AP is 2 years 3 months before the end of the preceding house (the Low Point (LP) of that house). Thus we have a significant change of psychological orientation, according to the houses, at ages around, or just before 4, 10, 16, 22, 28, 34, 40, 46, 52, 58, 64, 70,…

These changes of orientation happen without reference to other astrological features in the birth chart – this is a six-year psychological rhythm to life. We do not need to draw a birth chart to understand these changes of psychological orientation. Of course, using a birth chart, an astrologer can gain much more information about the psychological processes that are going on.

This Huber developmental theory has been shown by John Grove to correlate reasonably well with the similar developmental theory of psychoanalytic theorist Erik Erikson[8].

The first time around: Age 0-70

In *Life Clock* the Hubers give extensive treatment of the subject of age progression through each of the houses 1-12, and the implications of astrological features such as planets, signs, aspects, Low Points.

The 12th house completes the first cycle of the Life Clock. Its theme is the return from the outer world to the core of the self – detachment from the external world to turn inwards and explore inner dimensions. A certain isolation is required for this task, which may be voluntary or involuntary.

At this time we can usually become more detached since life is, for many, less demanding. We can turn to higher things, discover treasures within and learn how to be at one with ourselves.

The second time around: Age 70-90

In the following we summarise those parts of *Life Clock* that are particularly relevant to the second time around – the approach of the AP through the 12th house to the AC, and its subsequent progression through the first three houses for the second time[9].

---

[8] See Grove, John, *Life Passages*, HopeWell 2017, page 26 for comparison of Huber and Erikson developmental stages.

[9] Huber, Bruno & Louise, *Life Clock*, HopeWell 2006, 2022, pages 60, 106, 246-254

The approach to the AC: new challenge, new orientation

Age 70 represents the start of old age and the possible lessening of physical power. As we reach the 12th house Low Point, we are already psychologically preparing for passing over the AC and having our second encounter with the 1st house – a new beginning.

At LP 12 the person encounters a great life challenge: to find the way back to himself/herself and become wise. True character becomes more focused and more recognizable. Those who are selfless, loving, just, and generous are now even more so; those who are difficult, egotistical, hard, bitter, petty, suspicious, and argumentative calcify along these lines.

Finding our own particular style of life in old age is the test for the whole life, revealing what we have made of ourselves. Have we been able to reach maturity? The mentally balanced person becomes wise and shines with inner peace and kindness because nothing is wanted for the self. The end is viewed calmly as a necessary completion. We seek spiritual meaning in life. Wisdom is the ideal goal, but reached only by the few.

We are challenged to find our true selves, to become self-sufficient. This necessitates release from everything external that would imprison the self, so that a higher condition of soul may be born from the centre of being. A split is experienced between the desire to sit back and savour the fruit of achievement and the impulse to forget the joys and sorrows of the past and embrace life again like a carefree child. The result is often a spiritual rebirth which can carry us far over the AC again, or else can produce mere second childhood.

Aging can also give rise to unpleasant symptoms and illness or infirmity. A mentally sound, vital attitude and sensible body care can enable acceptance of life, the joy of living, the affection of others, and a still-functioning intact ego.

Return of the Age Point to Houses 1-3

When the AP returns to houses 1-3 our "little ego" should no longer be so important to us. It is more important to learn to identify with our soul/ Higher Self, freeing ourselves from old patterns and false and misleading notions, enabling us to fathom the deeper meaning behind life's pattern.

With good fortune, we can enjoy life's later years. They offer a repetition of experiences of childhood, but on a higher rung on the evolutionary spiral. Childhood memories may come back vividly, and we can "re-view" them from a more mature consciousness. There may be a new clarity of vision and understanding; perhaps a problem or trauma which had its origin in our early years (1st and 2nd houses) and/or 36 years later (7th and 8th houses) can now be seen with detachment, in perspective, and may find resolution.

Age Point in the 1st house (Aries energy): Age 72-77

A new start, a new way of being. Reawakening of the enterprising spirit, joie de vivre, struggle against restrictions, understanding available energies.

The 1st house gives a new start. The urge to manifest or begin anew can now be used creatively and to advantage, enabling us to carry on courageously and overcome limitations, weakness, lethargy, and defeatism. We know that we've made progress once we can accept that even our most painful experiences – rejection, failure, humiliation – were just what we needed at that time for our inner growth, by being shaken out of old attitudes and forced to some hard thinking. Now we can become consciously aware of our own inner core, of our own worth, without the need for affirmation by others.

At this stage some may yield to the temptation of letting themselves go, falling back on their little ego, loth to change anything. This stops further development. Others may overestimate their resources, and make wonderful plans, but then must concede that they are no longer young and need to ration their energies.

Now we should be able to see our ego from a more realistic perspective, but frequently this view can still be somewhat egocentric. Many become defiant and want to demonstrate their individuality. Those who lack any concept of the Higher Self may insist on competing with those around them, which is ultimately bound to fail as younger people will always have a physical advantage. In care homes, some residents can be obstreperous and cantankerous, unwilling to abide by basic regulations or consider helpful advice.

On this second turn of the spiral, the 1st house demands conscious awareness of the reality of soul and spirit. No longer is it important to assert our ego, to outshine others, to be seen to be the biggest and best. Instead, we must aim for self-awareness and for confirming our knowledge of our Higher Self. Key questions demand to be answered: "Who am I? What is my true reality? How can I best use the span of life left to me?" Maybe we can then tap into a higher source which will guide our spiritual destiny. We may experience a new zest for life, but it is important that this surge comes not from our little ego, but from our soul. Then we can do nothing but accept this and yield to its bidding. "Thy will be done O Lord, not mine." We then conclude that we have been given free will to affirm our Higher Self, which is most appropriately understood and expressed in religious or philosophical terms.

From Ascendant to LP 1: Age 72-75

Second "birth", renewed zest for life, spontaneous self

The Ascendant (AC) is symbolically the "zero-point," where we began life's journey. The second time around we again come in touch with transcendental dimensions for a possible new beginning. If we are so inclined, this becomes a spiritual rebirth. We are part of two worlds: the visible material and the invisible spiritual. We become conscious of this through crises around this time which demand a clear inner attitude.

At the AC we are new-born in a sense, receiving a jolt of vitality something like that at birth. Astrologically, we have a new and conscious perception and understanding of any planets in the 1st house. When these planets were transited in infancy, we were passive, unable to digest and work on our impressions or make our own decisions. Now we meet those planets again and can use this fresh encounter to reach a deeper understanding of our destiny and of ourselves. Entering the mutable first third of the chart, we can more easily adjust to changes.

The sign of the AC is particularly significant in astrological psychology as representing a goal direction for life, the meaning of our lives, qualities coming from the 'seed thought' for that sign[10].

In the 1st house we can experience rekindled confidence and re-awakened *joie de vivre*. Just as in spring buds burst forth after a long cold winter, so Aries' cardinal energy brushes aside anxieties, grief, depression, and unwarranted worry. We can say YES to life with renewed zest, feel more enterprising and healthier. Past worries or issues no longer have power over us; we can break through any restrictive habits and branch out into new territory. We can do what we want to do and realize long-held dreams. Some no longer want their lives to be ruled by other people's opinions, rejecting their advice as interference, developing an unexpected degree of courage, even becoming foolhardy.

When we reach LP 1 we may come more to our senses, now being confronted by the greater realism of the 2nd house. The 2nd house need for security begins to make itself felt. Here some will come into conflict with the world, rejecting advice as unwarranted interference and restriction; they can be stubborn and unreasonable, and it can be impossible to have a rational argument with them. They insist on making their own decisions regardless, ignoring their physical limitations. Their own children are often on the receiving end of this defiant attitude. In extreme cases there may be threats to disinherit children, leading to a power struggle between generations. But eventual defeat is unavoidable; they have to concede that they really aren't as young as they used to be!

---

[10] Ibid, page 187. See also Huber, Louise, *Reflections and Meditations on the Signs of the Zodiac*.

From LP 1 to cusp 2: Age 76-77

Renewal of family feelings

In this calming phase we must face up to our limitations and reconnect with others. Many become painfully aware of their dependence on others and prepare to eventually hand over. The 2nd house is showing its influence; we want to ensure our comfort and security, and cherish the feeling of belonging, so we learn to compromise and be amenable. Some are thrown back onto their own resources and may have to reap the consequences of past financial excesses.

Age Point in the 2nd House (Taurus energy): Age 78-83

Adapting to reality, relying on inner resources, working through childhood experiences, learning to detach from possessions and relationships, handling diminishing life energies.

In the 2nd house we learn to deal sensibly with available energies and material goods. We may make do with less, perhaps by restricting living quarters or by parting with things not really needed. Possessions accumulated over the years no longer bring joy but become a burden. We let go of once-treasured mementoes – not only material objects, but also some of our nearest and dearest. Erstwhile friends may die before our eyes, we grieve for past companionships and past times, feeling deserted. The 2nd house forces us to become aware of the impermanence of physical existence. Material concerns lose their importance when death beckons; we cannot take them with us. It is wise to distribute knick-knacks and valuables among heirs so they can't squabble about them later. The task is to part with them with good grace.

Some stubbornly hang on to everything with grim determination, becoming mean-spirited, hiding behind legal rights. Some even engage in power games. If they feel slighted by someone in the past, and haven't worked through this experience, they may make a point of paying them back – perhaps disinheriting non-favourite relatives as punishment. Such conduct is not conducive to peace of mind. This is the house of karma. The principle of cause and effect is directly related to the law of economy of the possession axis (2/8). "As you sow, so you shall reap." Peace of mind eludes us, and until we have balanced our karmic books we may suffer physical 'dis-ease.'

When the AP conjoins a planet in the 2nd house, we may relive childhood experiences. Some will turn these over and over in their minds, talking about them, repeating themselves endlessly. This repetition may give them a chance to come to terms with their traumas. Unfortunately, those around can find the whole process burdensome and difficult. This phase could be fruitful to help unravel old complexes and hang-ups, so it could be beneficial to use such occasions to try to bring about a reconciliation where there may have been disharmony. For instance, relatives caring for seniors can do a great deal to bring about a harmonious resolution of a karmic parent/child conflict.

Role reversals are common here. The parents may become needy, while the "children" must learn to parent their parents. Observing their parents' deterioration into helplessness and dependency demands a great deal of understanding from adult offspring, and a genuine wish to help, but, with a degree of detachment from their parents' condition, letting go of powerful father or mother figures which were previously so important.

Cusp 2 to LP 2: Age 78-81

Letting go, dreams and memories, working with childhood experiences

This is the house of letting go, but the 2nd house can also reignite a preoccupation with material possessions. Those of a materialistic frame of mind surround themselves with material goods and personal possessions; become tight-fisted, unwilling to part with anything. They are scared of being short-changed; won't share belongings; quarrel over trifles; become jealous and take all possible precautions lest anyone deprive them of anything. All manner of anxieties arise in this phase—fears of material, mental, or spiritual loss.

At LP 2 it is quite usual to experience a crisis through the unavoidable process of continuing detachment and loss – the loss of loved ones, a feeling of diminishing security or having to move away from familiar surroundings. We must face the fact that nothing lasts forever, neither possessions nor life itself. Only a spiritual viewpoint can help us to cope constructively, pointing the way to detach voluntarily from everything which up to then symbolized our material security.

Those who insist on hanging on to old habits – stubbornly continuing their old ways, rejecting change, afraid of uncertainty – could be much happier if only they'd let go.

LP 2 to cusp 3: Age 82-83
Fading of vitality

At this stage a spiritual perspective helps us to carry on meaningfully. We can gain new knowledge and awareness and find new interests, giving new impetus to our lives. Physical energies may decline, we may no longer be able to take part in everything that's going on around us, but it is important to keep an active mind. The 'stress zone' leading up to the 3rd house can stimulate mental activity and intellectual capacities. We can still take an active interest in all manner of things without needing to use significant physical resources. A lively interest in local affairs and maintaining social contacts is the best possible medicine to prevent deterioration.

Age Point in the 3rd House (Gemini energy): Age 84-89

Making friends with dwindling time, dissolving sense of identity, possible approaching senility, realizing the ephemeral nature of life, uncertainty, preparing for death.

Many people in this phase have moments of true illumination and intuition, suddenly seeming to fathom the deeper meaning of events and surprising others by their wisdom. At the same time, they often forget everyday affairs, because they no longer matter.

Others react to their 3rd house feelings of uncertainty and ambiguity with a cold optimism and indifference to any attempt to find meaning. They live from day to day without serious thinking; everything that used to be of value just evaporates. In the 2nd house they may have been frugal, steadfast, even stubborn; now these traits can just dissolve away.

This may no longer seem to be the same person. The change from a fixed to a mutable way of being is very pronounced at this stage.

During the identity crisis at LP 3, the ego can either become more ephemeral for the Higher Self to use, or it can ossify. Those who have developed awareness of their spiritual nature will take this opportunity to prepare consciously for the forthcoming transition. However, many do not cope well with this challenge as they are insufficiently prepared for it.

Unfortunately, our culture[11] does not deal with the process of dying with dignity. The personality, instead of becoming more fluid, often hardens because of overwhelming fear of death. Such people are no longer open to new learning, their consciousness already clouded while bodily functions are still intact. The closer they come to the IC, the more they are beyond caring.

Often people must be uprooted from home and familiar surroundings, perhaps moving into a care home when they can no longer look after themselves. For some, this may well be the end, as they cannot cope with such drastic change.

The transformation of ego into Higher Self demands conscious cooperation. That's why we should make sure that we are well acquainted with the process of dying and the nature of life after death, so that we know what to expect. Nowadays there are many books available on this subject.[12]

---

[11] *Life Clock* was first published in Switzerland in 1980, so the surrounding culture for the Hubers was the middle-Europe at that time.

[12] The Hubers quote books by Elisabeth Kübler-Ross (*On Death & Dying*, Simon & Schuster/Touchstone, 1969. and by Alice A. Bailey. (*Esoteric*

Cusp 3 to LP 3: Age 84-87

Musings, transformation, restitution; forming of ideas. Then identity crisis.

In this phase some people become more open to new ideas, even embarking on a new course of study. Just as between ages 12-16 we are busy attending school, we have a similar opportunity during the second passage of the AP through the 3rd house.

The year of LP 3 can create an identity crisis, because our sense of our selfhood is beginning to dissolve. We may have intellectual interests, but the volatile nature of this house tends to be detrimental for the personality. Many lose short-term memory, the days seem to merge into each other, powers of discernment are lost, as is the notion of the passage of time.

LP 3 to cusp 4: Age 88-89

Dissolution of sense of selfhood

The volatile principle of the 3rd house, of Gemini, can dissolve a person's feeling for space and time. The approaching 4th house cusp can dissipate the sense of self, to be engulfed by the collective. Events once deemed important vanish into the mists of time, forgotten. It doesn't seem to matter greatly whether it concerned oneself or someone else. The cardinal IC/MC axis which signalled the beginning of our individuation

---

Healing: The Process of Restitution, pages 460-485, and *A Treatise on White Magic: Salvation from the Fear of Death*, pages 492-507.) There are now many more books on death and dying, including Will Parfitt's *The Something and Nothing of Death*, Peter and Elizabeth Fenwick's *The Art of Dying*.

process now erodes the meaning of selfhood. Some people are able to drop further demands and expectations from life and prepare consciously for the process of dying.

In perspective

Of course, the Hubers were describing a general developmental process with astrological correlations over time. The developmental potential applies to everyone, but we should not suppose that this timescale should necessarily apply to any particular human being.

Chapter 3. What other authors say about this stage of life.

The Hubers in context

Whilst traditional astrology, and more traditional astrologers, look at old age or senior years in terms of planetary cycles, astrological psychology and the Huber Method uses Age Progression to focus on specific life phases from birth onwards. The emphasis is on what the individual may experience on an inner, psychological level as well as on the outer, physical level as they mature and their Age Point moves around the chart.

In more traditional astrological methods of timing, three Saturn return cycles, each of approximately 29 years, takes the age of the individual to 87 years, and one Uranus cycle marks 84 years of age. Both cycles coincide with when age reaches the 80s; they put ageing on the astrological map in a more general, non-specific way. Saturn, for example, is often identified astrologically as Old Father Time, ruling maturity and old age. In *The Planets Suite* by Gustav Holst, who studied astrology, Saturn is named as the Bringer of Old Age. Holst's music depicting Saturn reflects the slowness and stiffness of senior years, along with gravitas and a certain quiet serenity.

In 2008, *The Daily Mail* newspaper[13] reported a correlation between life experience and a specific life phase – that of the mid-life crisis. The Hubers had already discovered this years previously in their research on Age Progression. Researchers at

---

[13] https://www.dailymail.co.uk/news/article-510943/The-age-depression-44-marks-start-mid-life-crisis--scientists-say-lasts-years.html

Warwick University in Britain, and Dartmouth College in the United States, found that age 44 marks the start of the mid-life crisis. It was found that happiness and depression follow a U-shaped curve, the deepest trough of the curve occurring when people are approximately aged 44, saying "the low period does not lift significantly for several years".

In astrological psychology, when the Age Point reaches age 42, a period of mid-life crisis begins. In this phase we move through the Low Point of the 8th house and of the whole chart, the Low Point of life. A period of change of outlook, transformation and reorientation takes place, and continues for several years after this[14].

The scientists took it no further but the Hubers had already done so. The hand of the LifeClock continues to move on and when it reaches, at age 84 (one Uranus cycle and approximately 42/48 years after that Low Point) the Age Point of the individual will once again have travelled through the 2nd house of the chart, just as it did when they were between the ages of 6 and 12.

As children, when we were in the 2nd house, it's likely that books, toys and treasured possessions were of great importance to us. We identify strongly with them and want to hold on to them. "That's mine, give it back!" often heralds the start of a childhood squabble over a prized possession.

When we reach the 2nd house again, in our 80s, issues are likely to arise about our accumulated adult possessions. Savings and worldly goods are considered as we make a will, or give

---

[14] Bruno and Louise Huber, state in *Life Clock[14]* that "Between ages 42 and 48 the phase corresponds to what we call mid-life crisis".

away things we no longer require. Some people in this age group try to hang on tightly to what is theirs, fearful it might be taken away from them; others, who have learned to loosen their hold on material possessions, may be satisfied on a spiritual level by treasures of a more non-physical nature. They will let go far more lightly of what is no longer of relevance or importance.

Other astrologers

We looked at what various astrological authors have said about senior years and life beyond age 70, and a theme begins to emerge. Liz Greene[15] describes the Saturn and Uranus cycles, and suggests these often coincide with periods of crisis and reorientation. Howard Sasportas[16] says that in the 12th house where, using Age Progression, we turn 70 as we travel through the Low Point, "...the twin processes of the dissolution of the individual ego and the merging with something greater than the self is felt and experienced, not via the mind or intellect... but with our heart and soul". He suggests that in the 12th house we do not necessarily have to sacrifice things, but rather give up our attachment to them.

Errol Weiner[17] emphasises the importance of the sign on the Ascendant – the Rising Sign – and links it to the process of spiritual awakening, the "second birth". He discusses the significance of Saturn's cycles, focusing on the potential energy

---

[15] Greene, Liz, *Relating* pp 241-247
[16] Sasportas, Howard, *The Twelve Houses* pp 98 - 107
[17] Weiner, Errol, *Transpersonal Astrology: Finding the Soul's Purpose* pp110-111

of the Rising Sign, calling it "...the powerhouse – the central electromagnetic centre of one's life (chart) and this energy begins to be released when one awakens… when one awakens to new life one begins to evolve into spirit, for one's spiritual purpose, aspirations and goals begin to take hold." Weiner here draws upon the esoteric teachings of Alice Bailey's Arcane School and the Master DK. Bruno and Louise Huber were deeply involved with these teachings, which underpin much of their astrological psychology[18].

It is not altogether surprising, then, that at age 70 in the Hubers' Age Progression, the 12th house Low Point is navigated and experienced by the individual ahead of crossing over the Ascendant/Rising Sign for the second time. At age 72, this awakening may begin with the dawning and realisation of new insights and understandings, backed up by a lifetime of experience.

Dane Rudhyar[19] speaks of the process of identification with the purpose of the soul, which is relevant to this later stage of life. Rudhyar notes a change in values, often something which happens to people in their senior years. The individual is "...no longer as he was; his activities change – or, if outwardly the same, they begin to acquire a new quality of radiation and a new potency."

Roberto Assagioli – Looking within

As already mentioned, Roberto Assagioli, founder of Psychosynthesis and contemporary of Carl Jung, was Bruno &

---

[18] Hopewell, Barry & Joyce, *Piercing the Eggshell* pp33-40
[19] Rudhyar, Dane, *An Astrological Triptych* p227-228

Louise Huber's mentor as they developed astrological psychology.[20]

Assagioli[21] sees old age as a "critical age" when negative attributes and attitudes can set in if the individual withdraws from life around him or her. A balancing influence is needed to offset what he sees as a spiritual death, just as senility leads to physical death. Fortunately, other elements of life often intervene so that those on what might be a downward spiral, make a change of direction. Events and experiences change us by forcing us to look within and redirect our attention to higher levels of the spiral as we begin to set ourselves free from the illusions and attachments which hold us.

Assagioli says that when this happens, people can be imbued with a new sense of vitality, power and enthusiasm. "It is as if they had been rejuvenated: they have a new youthfulness within and the better characteristics of youth are added to those of maturity, without detracting from them." Bruno and Louise describe the return of the Age Point to the 1st house in a similar way[22]: "We can say YES to life with renewed zest, feel more enterprising, and also healthier. Many of the worries of the past no longer have power over us….".

James Hillman – Lasting to Leaving

Psychologist James Hillman[23] explores three main aspects of ageing, all relevant to life experiences when the Age Point is

---

[20] Hopewell, Barry & Joyce, *Piercing the Eggshell* pp45-56
[21] Assagioli, Roberto, *Transpersonal Development* p111
[22] Huber, Bruno & Louise, *Life Clock* p249
[23] Hillman, James, *The Force of Character and the Lasting Life*

moving through the 1st and 2nd houses of the chart, and beyond. He names them "Lasting", "Leaving" and "Left".

"Lasting", he says, "…means remaining true to form… what lasts is our character." We tap into the depth of our ancestry, recognising its riches and valuing what is "old", maybe becoming nostalgic by connecting with past memories and experiences which have helped form our character.

Moving from "Lasting" to "Leaving" brings changes in our psychological attitudes as we move from holding on, to letting go; what has previously been significant and important has outlasted its usefulness. Such attitudes "…can no longer sustain us, not because we are old, but because *they* are old. The need to hold on becomes a regressive resistance, spawned by fear of dying more than by zest for living".

And when we have "Left" those outworn attitudes behind, there arises a theme of giving back in later years as we become more involved in community matters and volunteer willingly to help out with causes close to our hearts. At this stage we respond and live our lives with more kindness and consideration to others and to the environment, having slowed down, allowing our true character to shine through.

Also highlighted by Hillman is the importance of grandparenting. There are beneficial links between the Age Points of both grandchildren and grandparents being in the same house, as they are able to share common ground. With their accumulated experience and wisdom, grandparents can offer a wealth of understanding, encouragement and support to the next generation.

Hillman acknowledges and includes the validity of astrology in his exploration of character and aging saying,

"Astrology offers a language of traits… the presentation of a heavenful of characteristics that refer the individual soul to archetypal powers… It speaks of character in images".

Will Parfitt – Acceptance

Will Parfitt, psychotherapist and teacher of psychosynthesis and Kabbalah, says that having a positive attitude towards growth throughout life is essential[24]. He says, "If we can keep this attitude right though life, an attitude of positive expectation, of expecting the best from life, then we age not only gracefully but also wisely."

On becoming an Elder, Will asserts that this is not defined by the age a person reaches, but how well they have integrated the lessons of life, suggesting that "…the truest sign of integration – and the wisdom that comes with it – is recognising that we are just right as we are…" This level of personal acceptance of who we are, by and for ourselves, is akin to experiencing life in the 1st house, but on a different turn of the spiral, and for the second time around.

Connie Zweig – Role to Soul

Retired psychotherapist Connie Zweig draws on her personal experience of being an Elder alongside her professional work with others, also Elders, travelling the path from role to soul [25]. She likens Elders to teachers or mentors, those who willingly pass on the wisdom of their life experience, not from a place of ego, or of needing recognition for their know-how,

---

[24]Parfitt, Will, *The Something and Nothing of Death* pp24-26
[25]Zweig, Connie, *The Inner Work of Age – Shifting from Role to Soul*

but simply because they are at ease with themselves ***just as they are*** and don't need to prove anything, or be how others might "expect" them to be. There is a shift from identification of self with a specific role. All association with that role is dropped as the individual moves towards a place of soul where attention is focussed and quiet and there is no need or pressure to do anything; the Elder can just "be".

Zweig suggests that Elders, behaving in this way, give hard-won knowledge to the next generation, welcoming a new generation of seekers and agents of change. The ego is set aside; it has no place when role or roles, which might have defined us during our more active working life are dropped, as the essence of soul begins to find its place. She says that we must be careful not to define being an Elder too tightly; there are many facets to being one, and she gives examples of what an Elder does not do: "… does not resist change and impermanence… does not need to be right… does not project a shadow character on to others… does not refuse to give his/her gifts to future generations..."

For some it is possible to be an Elder when still in their fifties, by hearing and responding to the soul's mission with authenticity and gravitas, but it is often in later years that this awareness and questioning of lifestyle and attitudes occurs. Going through the 12th house Low Point at 70 and, as the Age Point crosses the Ascendant for the second time at age 72, experiencing the 1st house anew and seeing life through awakened eyes is the more common experience; it is what we are focussing on in this book.

Zweig offers a word of warning though. We cannot assume that an Elder qualifies for this appellation if they are an

"...eighty-five-year-old who believes they are a victim and deserves revenge..." This she states quite clearly, is not being an Elder!

John Robinson – Conscious Aging

Psychologist John Robinson presents a similar story to Zweig, in terms of conscious aging: "aging and death are meant to expand our consciousness, grow our soul, and increase our ability to love, forgive, surrender, and meet death head on."[26] He also sees aging as the individual contribution to a collective transformation to a new world. This spiritual transformation requires a realisation of who we really are, and our hitherto separation from the divine core. We become a witness, rather than being "trapped in a mental thought-world." Our final task is facing our personal death. In engaging in this process we become Elders, as above.

Robinson's three secrets of aging[27] are, essentially:
1. releasing the past, who we were and all we have, stepping across the threshold into a new life.
2. transcending our habitual, thought-driven identity and way of life, and awakening mystical consciousness.
3. witnessing Divinity giving birth to the divine world moment-by-moment and take part in the unfolding of the Great Work.

Robinson suggests that an important part of this aging process is some sort of Life Review, answering questions such

---

[26] Robinson, John, *The Three Secrets of Aging*, O Books, 2012
[27] Robinson, Ibid, location 1357

as "What has my life been about? What happened to me? How did it turn out? What have I learned? …We don't have to rework all our wounds, just the ones that invite us back… Whatever regrets, failures, wounds, or guilt we still carry need to be faced, grieved, healed, and surrendered." We have to let go to move on.

It is notable that Huber Age Progression provides a potentially valuable tool to help in this process of Life Review, as discussed further in Chapter 6.

Chapter 4. Our survey

Research intention

In January 2022 we approached Huber contacts in the English, Spanish and German speaking worlds with a request for help in researching into real life experiences beginning with the Age Point's arrival at the Low Point of the 12th house, at age 70, and looking beyond this to the time when the AP moves through the mutable zone of the 12th house, approaches and crosses the AC, then passes through the 1st, 2nd, and 3rd houses for the second time.

The theory is well documented in Life Clock, as described in Chapter 2, but we were looking for real life experiences of what it's like being 70 and beyond, relating this to that theory.

Most of our respondents would already have an understanding of their personal experience of earlier AP transits through the houses. We were now interested in their further experiences, having reached these senior years at age 70+.

We also invited input from a selection of non-astrologers, where we could ourselves apply limited astrological interpretation.

The detailed guidelines we initially sent out, and a request for supplementary input related to the 36-year echo effect, are included in Appendix 2 on page 173.

4.1 Survey Analysis Overview

Most of the responses received were from UK or Central Europe:

- UK   12
- Germany/Switzerland   8
- Other Europe   3
- Rest of World   2
- Total   25

Most of the respondents were in the 1st house at the time of their submission:

- pre 1938 (in 3rd house, 84+)   1
- 1938-1943 (in 2nd house, 78+)   2
- 1944-1949 (in 1st house, 72+)   18
- 1950 on (in 12th house, 66+)   4

A significant number of respondents identified 'echoes' of experience with those 36 or 72 years previously[28]. 72 years corresponds to the 'same house' experiences in early life; 36 years corresponds to experiences when AP was in the opposite house.

- 72 years before   13
- 36 years before   6

---

[28] As the Age Point progresses around the chart it makes an aspect to each planet every 6 years. The most powerful connections are usually made at the 0° conjunction and 180° opposition aspects, i.e. every 36 years. Hence our specific focus on echoes of life experience over this period.

During the analysis we also noted correspondence of the respondent's psychological experiences with astrological features passed over by the AP:

- Change of sign through which the AP is passing, related to the quality of the person's life experience.
- Conjunction of AP with a planet, related to experience of those planetary energies and related aspect patterns.
- AP passing over the Low Point of a house.
- AP passing over a house cusp or the 'stress area' leading up to it.
- AP passing over the Crossing Point of the chart.

The following table shows the number of occurrences related to the 12th, 1st and 2nd houses respectively.

	12H	1H	2H
Sign change	16	5	1
Planetary conjunctionj	17	10	1
Low Point	23	3	0
Stress area/cusp	24	3	0
CrossingPoint	6	0	0

There were also a small number of references to Moon Node and House charts.

Given that we were interested in experiences, it is more meaningful to look at the stories told by these individuals related to their own charts. These now follow in Chapter 5.

Chapter 5. Selected stories

The following stories were supplied in response to the survey described in Chapter 4. They are grouped as follows:

> 5.1 Stories from the 12th house
> 5.2 Stories from the 1st house
> 5.3 Stories from the 2nd and 3rd houses

This grouping is somewhat arbitrary, as an individual story may include, for example, the 12th house LP, the AC and experiences in the first house including the LP. The stories themselves are more important than the grouping they have been placed in.

5.1 Stories from the 12th House

Many of our stories are about just beginning the journey over the AC and into the 1st house, having but a taste of it from LP 12 onward and over the AC.

> 5.1.1 Kerstin
> 5.1.2 Pam
> 5.1.3 Christin
> 5.1.4 Sue
> 5.1.5 Frieda
> 5.1.6 Uschi
> 5.1.7 Gabrielle
> 5.1.8 Katharina
> 5.1.9 Georgina and Paul
> 5.1.10 Elly
> 5.1.11 Trish

5.1.1 Kerstin

Kerstin was born in Sweden but has lived in England for many years. Her story from the 12th house cusp tells of dealing with early trauma, discovering that she is a Highly Sensitive Person, and becoming a UK citizen after Brexit.

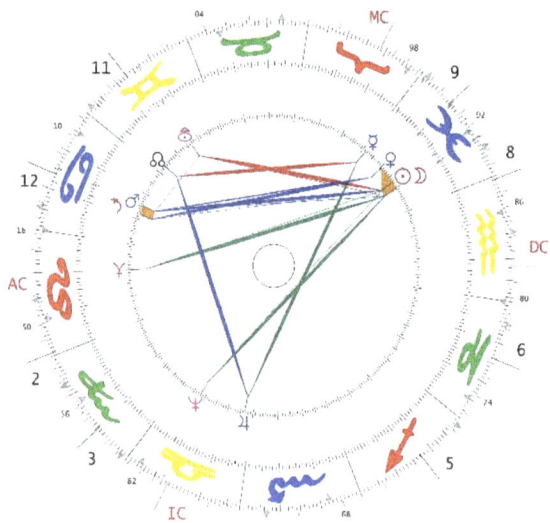

Figure 2 Kerstin 03.03.1946, 1300, Vaxjo, Sweden, 56N52 014E49

Saturn/Mars, Cusp 12, Crossing Point

AP was over Saturn/Mars, 12th house cusp and Crossing Point in June 2015. That's when I had my first appointment with Mary Aver. I'd had a feeling that I needed to find someone to talk to now and again – someone I didn't know. I already had lots of physical support (gentle, caring – Mars/Saturn trine Venus – regular aromatherapy, herbal/Ayurvedic medicine, cranial osteopathy, acupuncture). However, I realised I needed to draw towards me somebody to talk things through with as well. I'd heard Mary's name, but didn't know what she did. Anyway, I contacted her and went to see her for the first time in 2015. It turned out that she's a clairvoyant healer and therapist. It's been incredibly good to have her support while I've been going through the deep explorations of early trauma. Getting to know my body in a completely new way. To know, make friends with and trust it.

I was conscious that the AP was over the Crossing Point[29] as well and knew that I had to look deeply at my feelings about 'having a right to be here' (36 years before this is when Lisa, my first child was born – 3lb 1oz at birth, the size of a doll – the doll/transitional object that I lost when I was 5).

LP 12 and sign change to Leo

2 weeks before my 70th birthday Lisa sent me a link to a film by Dr Elaine Aron[30]. Lisa thought I might already be very knowledgeable about HSP (Highly Sensitive People), but I wasn't. Clive and I watched the film together and we both took the self-test on Elaine's website[31]. It turned out that I scored very highly for sensitivity, so I've spent a lot of time since then learning more about the trait and what research is being done. It's been totally life-changing for me and has helped both of us (and the rest of the family) understand what kind of person I am (and of course, most of the rest of the family are also HSPs.)

---

[29] Crossing Point – see Huber, Bruno & Louise, *Moon Node Astrology*, page 114.
[30] https://sensitivethemovie.com/
[31] hsperson.com

I have also been able to help clients, family and friends to learn to handle their sensitivity, while also appreciating the gifts that come with the trait. In fact, it took some time before I could really see the gifts for myself, as I was so conscious of the challenges that come with it.

AC and Pluto

I've been exploring my relationship with this earth and my physical body and have managed (with a lot of help) to make a new and loving relationship with this marvellous body that I've been blessed with. It hasn't always been easy – in fact in the Autumn of 2020 I went through several months of debilitating digestive problems, when AP was going over Pluto for the 2nd time. I did some deep trauma work around that and re-visited my first days as an embryo, realising that I was not wanted by my mother, so if I was going to 'make it' it was up to me to hang on. I'd had this insight a few years earlier, but now, I could acknowledge that I had actually chosen life myself. I was not a victim to a non-welcome womb, but an agent in my own life. A very important shift of emphasis. I feel I want to say plutonic in energy.

Going back to the Saturn/Mars AP transit, I feel that it reverberated for a couple of years before and after. I am struggling with my system being so sensitive, and I need to be cognisant of how I meet life on a daily basis, so that I don't get overwhelmed by all the energies that I pick up – both from those near me, and also from the collective and indeed cosmic. I'm grateful for the trines between Saturn/Mars and Sun/Moon/Venus as I'm aware of how these have helped me meet the challenges with more ease and gentleness (Pisces/Mutable and Cancer/Cardinal) than it could have been.

Stress area before AC

In 2016 I became a grandmother for the first time. This was so important and life transforming. I was actually present and helping with the birth (at home). I feel strongly that the role of elder and grandparent is so important, especially at these changing times – to help 'hold' these old souls who are coming in to help the world go through the evolutionary changes that we are in.

At this time I applied for UK Citizenship, a deep process in itself, taking 9 months. The ceremony was on the 28th of September 2017 only a couple of degrees before the AC. After this I felt a sense of calm and having landed, that I had never felt before. So, now, I even have a right not only to be on earth but also to stay in the country I chose to settle in.

During the years while AP went over the AC we've been lucky and blessed to welcome 3 more souls into the family, grandchildren.

Daughter and her partner both got Covid just after we'd all met to celebrate a 1st birthday in early March, but interestingly no one in the family was infected by them. The whole Coronavirus collective journey took up a lot of my time as I was trying to find my own relationship to it and not just fall into the collective narrative of fear and having to fight it.

This has again deepened my understanding of how we fit into the cosmos and are co-creators with everything else (including cells, viruses, plants, animals, stars, planets and so on). Not forgetting the Divine Spark/Source/God/Goddess/the

All-that-Is. Meditation and contemplation takes up more and more of my day.

Physical exercise has changed from quite hard-going tough pushing the body to a much gentler daily Yoga and walking in nature. It's so wonderful that the Feminine Principle is coming through more and more in different areas of life. Just what is needed for our survival.

LP 1

On the 11th of March we were woken up by a phone call (which should not have come through as my phone was on airplane mode) from a friend who told us that one of our closest friends had suddenly died of a heart attack. A true shock for the whole family as she was like an extra mother to the girls and grandchildren. This happened when my AP is conjunct Pluto. I managed to get to the funeral, but then became ill with covid.

5.1.2 Pam

Pam has spent most of her life in USA and has had a varied career, including being astrologer, attorney, priest and residential retreat manager. Her submission covers her retirement phase moving up to the AC. It is in note form.

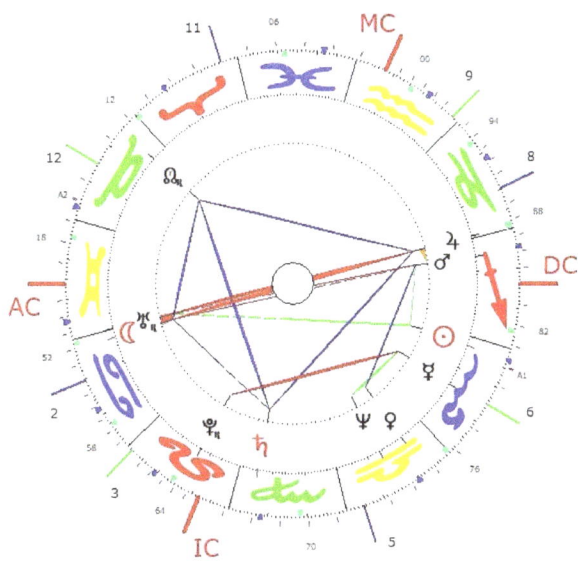

Figure 3 Pam, 19.11.1948, 1732, Ankara, Turkey

LP 11 to LP 12 − Gradual retirement

Survival Axis 6-12. Planets in 6th (Sun, Mercury in Scorpio) none in 12th. Keeping everyone out of Covid's way. Saying goodbye to professional associations. Workplace becomes a home hospital. Extended family/brother major illness survival challenge magnified later by Covid.

LP 11 AP entry into Taurus
Taurus: Generating money, land, fruit trees, plants. Renovating functional structures, purchasing income producing property, managing resources for brother/extended family. Domestic cooking, housekeeping, entertaining. Fine food/wine/silver. As AP moved toward Gemini: Intellectual desire to be let go of possessions: art, antiques, furniture. But struggled to do so. Taurean attachment/strings tied to stuff came as a surprise.

Mid 12th house entry to Gemini
Dealing with sibling, managing estates and trusts, cataloguing personal library, teaching/taking adult education Great Books courses. Active participation in political process/canvassing, reading daily news assiduously, lots of 'short distance' trips back and forth to doctors, classes. Intellectual commitment to learning more about diversity, racial bias, and especially white privilege.

Sudden email connections with 1st college love relationship (1967) and last romantic relationship before entering 'church' straitjacket (1983) and marriage in 2007.

Gemini AC's Esoteric ruler is Venus. Call to transcendent impersonal agape love. Mercury AC ruler square Pluto accurately describes the lifelong sibling tension now requiring harmonization.

LP 11 - Cul de Sac Aug 12 2012
Gradual retreat from high profile 11th house social life and engagement in world as Owner/ Manager San Geronimo Lodge and St. James Episcopal Church in Taos.

AP entered Taurus Aug 24 2012. Taurus husband died in early September. Suddenly, all things Taurean fell to me. Management of business, sale of property, estate planning, oversight of renovation/reconstruction projects, IRS Audit, cultivation of Lodge vineyards and Florida home landscape design.

AP trine Jupiter. Pilgrimage to Spain with parishioners. Spiritual experience in Cordoba.

AP conjunct North Node in pre-cusp area of 12th. Triggered Kite formation.

AP opposition Mercury 30 September 2014. Death of Mother.

Pilgrimage to India. Overwhelmed by poverty and own respiratory health in India.

***AP Cusp 12** November 2014 Retirement phase in full swing.*
Retreat from full time leadership and professional responsibilities.

Travel to Guatemala to officiate at cousin's daughter's wedding. Theological contretemps with bride's Catholic in-laws who were horrified that a female priest was officiating at their son's wedding. Moreover, honoring the couple's explicit wishes, I wrote a liturgy that honored the diverse community of friends in attendance.

AP opposite Balance Point Sun 2016
Sold San Geronimo Lodge. Moved back to Florida. Began substantial renovation of home for 'aging in place' plus purchased two adjacent homes creating family compound.

Served as my own general contractor/interior designer. Made some mistakes but not big ones!

Summer of 2016, 2017 and 2018 took last short term clergy positions for priests going on sabbatical.

AP enters Gemini, Fall 2017 Book-a-holics united.
Long time 40 year platonic/intellectual friend Jay became tenant in my house. Renovated separate building as office and library for our collective book collection. Joint active participation in Great Books literature classes in person and later on zoom. Astrology book re-read and purge.

Pilgrimage to Scotland. Visit to see the API Huber friends the Hopewells and Dick (Richard) Llewellyn

Pilgrimage to the Holy Land and Jordan with Presiding Bishop and close priest friend.

LP 12 August 2018
Stopped attending church regularly. Spent greater time with secular community.

My home became the hospital: Caregiving for bankrupt brother's extended household. Two 77 year old family members with life threatening disease and an adult schizophrenic.

2019 Walking meditations, Intense reading astrology, history, constant family crisis .

2020 Staying close to home of necessity due to Covid and family health issues. Continued activity reading literature and history. Back to university experience. (Progressed Sun, Mars and Mercury in 9th)

Became a political activist for Biden election.

Age 72, AP conjunct AC, November 2020 - Sextile Pluto and Moon.

Preparing to go back into the world. Elected to Board of Advisors for University of South Florida's Osher Life-Long Learning Institute. Commitment to education on diversity and ways of promoting civil discussions with difficult people. Continued reading of serious literature.

Moon Node Chart AP sextile Uranus November 2021

Taught my first history of astrology course (for non-astrologers). Astrology consultations via ZOOM expanding.

Domestic responsibilities for large household/extended family continue. Brother's partner dies, but extended family issues persist.

AP opposition Mars December 2021

Personal health issues age-related. Cataract surgery, melanoma surgery on arm/chest/nose.

Declined request that I run for local office of City Commission and Mayor.

Formal retirement from the Florida Bar (Law license) and the Episcopal Church.

5.1.3 Christin

Christin describes a closing of horizons during her period in the 12th house, but sees new beginnings as she enters the 1st house for the second time.

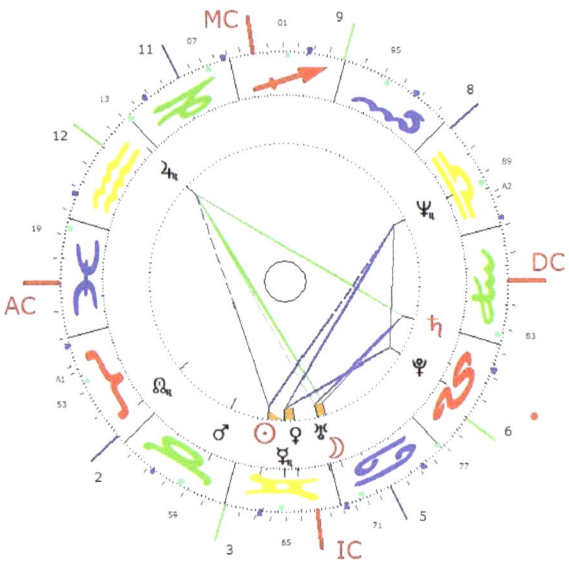

Figure 4 Christin, 30/05/1949, 0135, Biel, CH

Background

I had a good life, apart from my youth. My mother died of breast cancer in Dec 1951. Perhaps her illness is "the cause" that I am very reserved when it comes to contacts? All my friends live relatively far away, we only have contact by phone. In 1954, my father married my stepmother. The family constellation was difficult and full of conflict. In 1958 my half-sister was born - she was my living doll and also something like an oasis in this family.

I was the 3rd daughter – a disappointment for my parents, who had wanted a son. My father was a hotelier with heart and soul, my stepmother helped. I would have liked a family that had more time, that had more conversations, that had accompanied me more. The death of my father and stepmother didn't really shape me.

The time between 1961 and 1967 was stressful. I was overtaxed at school, had to deal with my profession, finally learned to be a medical laboratory assistant, not out of conviction, but because it was the shortest training period.

In 1968 I fell in love, we got married and in 1971 our daughter and in 1974 our son were born. Looking back, I say that I started living with the family.

12th house

It is notable that my zodiac signs match fairly closely the corresponding houses in my chart.

I have been in the 12th house since 2015. Yes, a retreat began. In 2016 I finished my work as an Ayurvedic therapist. This activity was a highlight in my life. I massaged many people for 20 years, sometimes on a monthly basis. Deep relationships of trust developed.

My husband became increasingly demented. I cared for him more and more, which increasingly isolated me. I left the pan flute group. Then came the covid pandemic. This time helped me, there were no activities, "everyone" stayed at home. Even when the measures were relaxed, I could do "home office" without any problems. A long-standing image (since about 1976) in me is "I want to be a tree" – only I was never clear how to implement this image. Now I am living it!

I was much affected by the death of my girlfriend in Nov 2019 (LP 12 in Pisces since Feb 2019). I still miss her very much, but feel her presence.

AC and looking forward

In 2021 I reached the AC. On my birthday, my colleagues played a pan flute concert in a castle garden. It was THE birthday for me! A NEW BEGINNING! I am very excited about what will happen again and how I will experience it.

Since about half a year I feel that there is a new ME coming into being, an impatience too. Is this Aries working? The first house? Or am I simply getting tired? I ask myself more and more often how long I want to be a private nurse? But I don't yet know what I would like to do if I were on my own...

Due to current politics, I also feel a fear that inhibits me from planning any kind of future. I think the "fat years" are over.

I have understood that my life fits exactly with my horoscope, or vice versa, I have made peace with my parents, I am in harmony with myself and my life. I have the confidence that my children and grandchildren will also make their way, that they too will meet the right people at the right time.

I have always been involved with esotericism (since giving birth in 1971) and questions of faith are always current. The topics around death/rebirth/ancestral energy are more or less present throughout life. They are more topical again now, because my husband, born in 1932, is very weak. Whether after his death I will look after people in a home for hours or massage their feet is a thought, but only a seed. I have a blue/green aspect pattern, which has given me the necessary peace. In the house chart I have red/blue. That's why it will be important for me to go out among people.

5.1.4 Sue

Sue Lewis[32] was a long-time member of the English Huber School and author. Sue describes her insightful journey from 12th house LP into the 1st house, reflecting back on earlier periods of her life and her gradual realisation of the freeze trauma she suffered from.

LP 12, 31 March 2019

In comparison with 2018 when my partner Terry and I travelled extensively, 2019 was subdued, as the AP dipped to LP 12. Nevertheless, we had a wonderful fortnight in the Dodecanese in May 2019, anticipating my 70th birthday in July. The following year we were grounded.

During the early summer of Covid lockdown in 2020, with AP semi-sextile my optimistic natal Jupiter, stimulated by a Jupiter return in first-house Capricorn, we kept safe and suffered little from the restrictions. With improved air quality in London, more birdsong, relaxed lunches on the roof terrace and pleasant weather, Terry and I enjoyed each other's

---

[32] See Sue Lewis, *Astrological Psychology, Western Esotericism, and the Transpersonal* (HopeWell, 2015), pp. 129-46, and articles: "Introvert/Extrovert on the Encounter Axis, Opening Doors: Surrealism, Cruelty, Incest and Catharsis", *Conjunction* 68, December 2017, pp. 4-12; "The Threefold Personality, Retrograde Learning Triangles, Growth, Self-Integration, Psychosynthesis and Eris", *Conjunction* 70, December 2018, pp. 8-11; "Disidentification, Planetary Watchers, Interconnectedness and our current crisis", *Conjunction* 73, July 2020, pp. 7-17; "All About Saturn", *Conjunction* 75, June 2021, pp. 20-27; "Rediscovering Sunlight in an Irritation Triangle", *Conjunction* 76, December 2021, pp. 6-13.

company. Independently we read and zoomed, expanding our inner horizons.

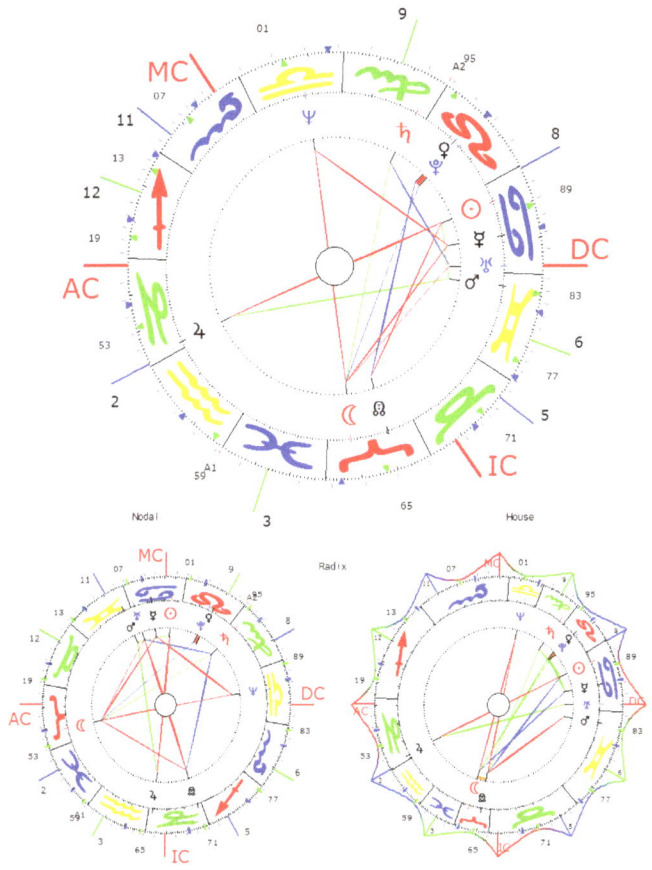

Figure 5 Sue Lewis, 16 July 1949, 19:45 BST, London, England—Nodal, Natal and House Charts

Age Point enters Capricorn, 23 November 2020

The idyll ended abruptly on 20 November 2020, when my email was hacked. Rainwater leaked into my wardrobe from the roof terrace of the flat above. Transiting Pluto reached 23°

Capricorn, opposing natal Sun at 23°52 Cancer. Sun opposes natal Jupiter at 27°47 Capricorn, and Jupiter is stressed just before the cusp of the 2nd house of possessions in the final degree of earth sign Capricorn. Jupiter holds a prominent position: Huber astrological psychologists call it the Tension Ruler[33]. A Tension Ruler spreads its influence over the hemisphere where it resides - in my chart, the "I" side, where it influences my identity, self-confidence, and personal space. Because of Jupiter's imposing position, the challenges posed by transiting Pluto hovering over my Sun/Jupiter opposition, throughout 2020-2024, are too intimately involved with my unfolding drama at the beginning of the 1st house to be ignored.[34]

Not being consciously materialistic, I may have paid insufficient attention to the Cancerian need to feel comfortable and safe at home. Assaults on my identity and property in early 2021 are described in detail in *Conjunction 76*. Covid spread, roads were busy, disgruntled Londoners on narrow pavements ignored social distancing, and Terry hibernated in his flat—a distant 10 minutes away from mine—until we were vaccinated in April. As I fought my corner, Alice Bailey's esoteric seed thought for Cancer had never felt more poignant: "I build a lighted house and therein dwell".

---

[33] Tension Ruler. Others prefer Bucket Handle—a term coined by American astrologer Marc Edmund Jones.
[34] Some scientists, who demoted Pluto to a dwarf in 2006, have questioned the wisdom of their decision since a fly-by in 2015 returned photographs showing an astounding level of activity on this icy little planet at the edge of our solar system. Few astrologers question the transformative impact of Pluto, individually and collectively.

During the early months of 2021, I kept sane by zooming online talks. I learnt about freeze trauma from a lecture on Polyvagal Theory that mentioned Peter A. Levine's *Waking The Tiger: Healing Trauma* (1997).[35]

Crossing the AC, July 2021

Roofers worked on the terraces above, beside and below my flat on my 72nd birthday, so Terry and I had a modest meal indoors. As AP crossed the Ascendant (AC) it opposed potentially explosive natal Uranus on my Descendent (DC). It was hot, tension was rising, and my patience was tested severely. A week later squally rain fell, new leaks showed up weaknesses in the roofers' work, while the workmen made themselves scarce and sent a mate to call at my front door demanding undocumented extra cash. My patience snapped. As my enraged tiger awoke, Terry arrived on cue to rescue me.[36] Something monumental shifted in my psyche and between us. I realised I had been suffering from freeze trauma since 1955, when my previously loving father fell ill and we ceased to communicate.

Maybe I could have broken free in 1971, when I retrieved my early memories, but the outpouring of love, integral to my

---

[35] William Bloom, "Polyvagal Theory and the Soul's Journey", Scientific and Medical Network (SMN) online lecture, 9 June 2021.

[36] C. G. Jung's astrology experiment demonstrated the longevity of couples when one partner's Sun is in conjunction with the other partner's Moon. Terry's Sun at 8° Aries is exactly conjunct my Aries Moon in the same degree. Although we neither live in the same flat nor always do the same things, we have been in partnership since March 1999, which is 24 years at the time of writing, and our relationship has deepened since my release from freeze trauma.

breakthrough in understanding, was rebuffed by the man who lit the touchpaper. Coping mechanisms were activated and full recovery put on hold.[37] In 2021 my partner was with me, and the new AP cycle is truly a rebirth. Rediscovering one's range of emotions, vulnerability and resilience in one's early seventies is daunting, greatly welcomed but scary. I am more spontaneous and alive than I can ever remember having been, and in a big hurry to make up lost time.

Uranus on the DC in Cancer occupies the reactive angle of a Large Learning Triangle with Saturn in Virgo (sextile) and Moon in Aries (square), a quincunx between Moon and Saturn forming the third side. AP on the AC temporarily converts a mutable learning triangle into a quadrangular fixed figure in my Natal Chart resembling a similar configuration in my Nodal Chart. The Nodal Chart is a mirror image, a glimpse into the prenatal past and the karma brought into this life for resolution. Saturn, the planet of memory, resides in the 8th house of transformation in both charts, a whirlpool of angst combined with associative memory, analytical skill, and a capacity for arbitration.[38] Saturn at the confluence of harmonious blue and

---

[37] Mother was wonderfully supportive, never possessive. Without her, I would not have survived the crisis of 1971, but she always knew that I needed the right man to unlock some part of me that had shut down.

[38] For Saturn and memory, see Bruno Huber, *Astrological Psychosynthesis: The Integration of Personality, Love and Intelligence in the Horoscope* (HopeWell, 2006), pp. 42-47. Saturn is both the exoteric and the esoteric ruler of my Capricorn AC, and the planet in my Crossing Points of 1959 and 1995. In 1959, a year after Father's death, my half-brother, Lyn, married and emigrated to Canada. A year later, Mother and I moved, leaving the house and garden of my childhood. A few months later I went to boarding school. So there were many significant changes in my young

consciousness-raising green aspects is my trouble-shooter. The 1st house corresponds to the "Awakening 'I'", and my first task in the second cycle is to clear the residue of a traumatic past in preparation for whatever calls me. I discussed my Large Learning Triangle in *Conjunction* 70 and 75, referenced in a footnote above. Learning triangles bring challenges into perspective and facilitate their resolution. Some operate quickly, while others—like mine—take the long route. Healing comes with perseverance. Learning triangles are facilitators of growth pioneered by the Hubers. Provided we remain open to possibilities and consciously aware, we keep on growing.

36-year echoes

During 2022, I followed several online courses on trauma with Gabor Maté, Richard Schwartz, Alex Howard, Thomas Hübl and others. Numerous insightful courses and conferences—some free—are accessible online for whoever is ready to receive them. Sometimes the wealth of information becomes a glut, and then a selective, discerning approach is needed to avoid being overwhelmed.

While processing this new material, I looked back at the AP's half cycle in the 1980s, focusing on the houses of work and partnership. I was 36 in 1985: unmarried, childless, stressed, and unfulfilled. In a pressured environment, an administrator told me I was "the little girl who looks after the

---

life. By 1995 I had settled into the most enjoyable and rewarding job of my administrative career. I participated in a deeply probing psychodrama course run by Marcia Karp at Cortijo Romero in Southern Spain. With experienced guidance I regressed to 1971, and I emerged with deeper understanding and greater strength to move forward.

boss while other people do the real work." That is one of those insults a woman never forgets.

From 1978, I combined employment as a personal assistant with out-of-hours study for a Diploma of the Faculty of Astrological Studies, successfully completed in 1981. I participated in weekend workshops on Transpersonal Psychology, Psychosynthesis, Kabbalah, Shamanism and much else. I trained in astrological counselling then, and again later when I became a Huber astrologer, but, although I am a keen observer of life, I have never felt comfortable in the counselling role for reasons that have only recently become clear. A person suffering from freeze trauma is disconnected from her emotional self and struggles to create a compassionate space in which to hold consultations. I could simulate but I was performing a role. As an astrologer, I preferred tutoring distance-learning students and running small groups where I would present a topic and encourage everyone to share experiences and insights.

In the late 1980s, I was invited to tutor Spanish students for the Faculty of Astrological Studies Certificate and thrilled when one of my students achieved first prize in 1988 and went on to become a leading light in the Spanish Huber School. I was also encouraged to research astrological symbolism in medieval Spanish literature, and had a paper published in 1999. Much as I welcomed these opportunities and had some success, they were hugely demanding side-lines and could not alleviate my mounting stress.[39] Nor did a stagnating relationship prevent

---

[39] Although I realised in 1971 that I could not sustain my previous level of intellectual activity while caring for my emotional and mental health, and

me from sliding into emotional meltdown in 1988. During the period leading up to and following my 36th birthday I was so stressed in my career and stuck in my emotional life that I involuntarily became one of the problems in a tense working environment that I eventually left. It took several changes of job and an invigorating but short-lived affair to get my life back on track.

Approaching 1st house Balance Point, opposition Mercury in Cancer, and square Neptune in Libra, October 2023

As I write in May 2023, I am discovering a range of emotions of which I had been unaware, accessing wider perspectives, and expanding my intuitive intelligence. While recognising some innate vulnerabilities, I am more integrated and resourceful, and profoundly grateful for a loving partnership that makes all the difference. Yes, I and my property have been challenged. Some but not all these issues have been resolved. This is an ongoing process. Disruptive, revelatory, and transformative transiting Pluto hovers around the cusp of Capricorn and Aquarius, bringing weaknesses and deceptions to light. Although my domestic upsets are a tiny speck in humankind's macrocosmic drama, they must be processed and shared, not swept back under the carpet.

---

was frequently irritated with myself for not being on top of my game, only in 2006 did I fully appreciate the extent to which various crises and setbacks had fragmented my mind. I was participating in an immersive psychosynthesis course during which I volunteered myself as a client. Something arose in that session about mind coordination and all at once I knew. Since then I have been working hard to synthesise my understanding and increase my speed of response. Terry has remarked on the improvements.

With AP in the first zone of the 1st house in the second cycle, finally released from freeze trauma, I am reworking some old stories one more time in a bid to let go of the shame that has dogged my recovery from adverse childhood experience and subsequent emotional crises.

As an introspective 16-year-old, I resonated to the lines from John Milton's *Paradise Lost*[40]: "The mind is its own place and in itself / Can make a heaven of hell, a hell of heaven". Mother's favourite mantra was "mind over matter", and she was a most courageous woman. It is our responsibility to confront our demons and make the most of life. I have taken my responsibilities so seriously that I shouldered a burden of guilt for asking Father challenging questions at the age of 5. Retrieving this memory sixteen years later, I knew I had shocked him into recognising how irresponsibly he had been behaving with his little daughter, and triggered a crisis in his heart condition. With Mother's tender loving care he recovered somewhat, surviving for another four years, but our communication channel was irrevocably broken. Freeze trauma became my defence, and residual unfinished business would find occasions to go into replay later in life. I now gather that it is common for children frozen out by a parent to blame themselves. To recover fully requires letting go of shame and becoming more self-compassionate. For me, this is work in progress.

Since 1970-71, I have known we are all part of a greater consciousness. That year I had opted to write a special subject

---

[40] John Milton's *Paradise Lost* (1667): bk 1, l. 254.

on the Theatre of the Absurd. As the walls of my study-bedroom metaphorically caved in on me, I endeavoured to understand the descent of Stéphane Mallarmé's *Igitur* down a winding staircase to a crypt, to commit philosophical suicide among ancestral tombs. What had this to do with the interactive dramas in Parisian pocket theatres where I had attempted to prepare for this course? Why was I hammering against an impregnable stone wall, desperate to be free? To break out of this negative spiral, I made conscious efforts to socialise. I became aware that other people in my vicinity were, perhaps unconsciously, complicit in steering me towards an approaching breakthrough in consciousness. I did not, in the end, write a special subject on Mallarmé's unactable poetic drama but, over the past few years, I have revisited this enigmatic world and the descent of Orpheus, supported by helpful reading.[41]

The French professor who ran our special subject group directed me to compare Antonin Artaud's *Les Cenci* (1935) – the archetype of Artaud's Theatre of Cruelty, which makes minimal use of dialogue for maximum dramatic effect – with Shelley's longer poetic drama based on a record of the Cenci family in a Roman archive recounting a tale of incest, cruelty and murder. I would never have chosen to study this unpleasant story but somewhere, in the recesses of my unconscious, it

---

[41] Two pertinent texts are: Robert D. Romanyshyn, *The Wounded Researcher: Research with Soul in Mind* (Abingdon, Oxon and New York: Routledge, 2021) and Robert McGahey, *The Orphic Moment: Shaman to Poet-Thinker in Plato, Nietzsche, and Mallarmé* (New York: SUNY, Albany, 1994).

jolted hidden memories, exactly as the dramatist intended, but not in a way that was helpful to the project.

Struggling at every level, I arranged an appointment with a more approachable tutor, who detected tensions in my writing and offered advice on clearing my desk and taking control of my work. On leaving his room, I felt his eyes powering through my body and turned to meet them. The *coup de foudre* of a cheap romantic novel! But this was serious, for me at least. As I started to put his academic advice into action, I had a flashback to the age of 4, the first of several lucid dreams of early childhood I would experience over coming months.[42] I wept for two days and went home at the weekend. Mother listened, she knew my recollections rang true.

As the tutor opted out of further involvement, I recalled a session with a palmist-clairvoyant two years previously, when he visualised this scenario and offered assurance that the right man would come to me. Mother had set up this consultation during the Easter break in 1969. The palm reader was a retired doctor, who had developed clairvoyant skills after his wife died. The session was confusing because my account of outer events, like the death of my father when I was 9 years old, did not tally with his conviction that I had suffered a tragic loss a few years earlier. Nor could I relate to his vision of the future. Mother was disappointed because nothing coherent had emerged, and I forgot about it. Two years later, the flashbacks to events when I was 4 and 5 years' old recalled to mind how the consultant

---

[42] For my transits and Age Point in 1971, see Joyce Hopewell, *Using Age Progression: Understanding Life's Journey* (Knutsford, HopeWell, 2013), pp. 68-69.

had homed in on a great loss at an early age. That and some other enigmatic points suddenly made perfect sense. If his interpretation of my past was accurate, then maybe he was right about the future as well. I wanted to believe that my man would come. More compellingly, I needed to believe so that I could find my way out of the tunnel and not be left stranded half way. Later I would painfully accept that my wish-thoughts had interfered with the clairvoyant session, and I was very self-recriminating.

Earlier this month, I listened to an online talk by the historian of alternative spirituality, Mitch Horowitz, on parapsychology and intention. Citing J. B. Rhine's *Extra-Sensory Perception* (1934), he said that ESP works best in conditions of hopeful expectancy and relaxation.[43] My intuitive perception of the need for hope to facilitate memory recall had been fundamentally sound, even though I would later have to pick up the pieces of my shattered hopes and expectations. There was, perhaps, no other way. So a warm embrace to thank my mercurial trickster sub-personality for keeping tenuous hopes alive in dire circumstances is long overdue. As a seeker of truth, I reluctantly acknowledge that sometimes we have to dissemble to get to the next stage of our journey.

Last week, Lissa Rankin gave a wonderful talk on combining conventional, alternative, and sacred medicine.[44] Of particular relevance to my story were her comments that coping mechanisms hamper growth and that we may have to break

---

[43] "What Parapsychology Reveals about the Powers of Intention", Mitch Horowitz, Institute of Noetic Sciences, 5 May 2023.
[44] "Sacred Medicine: Grounded for Hope in Optimal Healing Outcomes", Lissa Rankin MD, Scientific and Medical Network, 24 May 2023.

down completely before we can experience the benefits of post-traumatic growth. In the early 1970s, doubly wounded by tragic revelations from the past and unreciprocated love, I had to pull myself together, successfully complete a degree in modern languages, take a graduate/linguist/secretary training, and find a job. The head of my university student health centre had suggested to me that I made everything up and offered tranquillisers, which I refused. Mother believed in me and validated my story. I needed her, and we needed each other. So I had to cope and do my best to be relatively successful. It was perhaps inevitable that I would break down in 1988, when AP was half-way through the seventh house of partnerships, and perhaps I should not be so ashamed of failing to work through and integrate all my parts first time round.

My recovery leapt forward in November 1995 when I participated in an intensive week of psychodrama with experienced practitioners with whom I relived and transformed my experiences of 1971. This took place during my second Crossing Point when AP was in the 8th house conjunct natal Saturn, while transiting Uranus was in the 1st house in opposition to Sun and conjunct Jupiter. Stressed Jupiter and angular Uranus are influential planets in my Natal Chart and they inter-communicate through a consciousness-raising quincunx in my House Chart – hatching ideas, responding to hunches and making bold decisions. Both planets are currently transiting in Taurus, interacting with the Capricorn/Cancer oppositions that are most formative during these early years of the second AP cycle. A combination of Jupiter's vision and Uranian intuition with Taurean pragmatism can be constructive.

I have started reading Lissa Rankin's book, *Sacred Medicine*, with a foreword by Gabor Maté, whose *The Myth of Normal: Trauma, Illness and Healing in a Toxic Culture* (2022) I read and reviewed last year. In our turbulent world, the building of bridges between conventional and alternative medicine, and taking time to listen to those who are suffering, are significant developments in healing. I end here with three of Rankin's "Paradoxes of Healing" that I find particularly meaningful:[45]

- You can heal yourself *and* you can't do it alone.
  [This is fundamental to my understanding of life.]
- Lead with your heart *and* use your head.
  [Echoes of Blaise Pascal, "Le coeur a ses raisons, que la raison ne connaît point", a philosopher on my curriculum in 1971.[46]]
- We are not our bodies, our emotions, or our identities, *and* we are all those things.
  [Echoes of Roberto Assagioli, the father of Psychosynthesis, with whom the Hubers' worked as they conceived their astrological psychology.]

The second cycle may come with many challenges but it is also full of hope.

---

[45] Lissa Rankin, *Sacred Medicine: A Doctor's Quest to Unravel the Mysteries of Healing* (Boulder: Sounds True, 2022), pp. 8-9.
[46] "The heart has its reasons of which reason knows nothing", Blaise Pascal, *Pensées* (1654-62), pt 4 no. 277.

5.1.5 Frieda

Frieda describes her experience of passing through the 12th house.

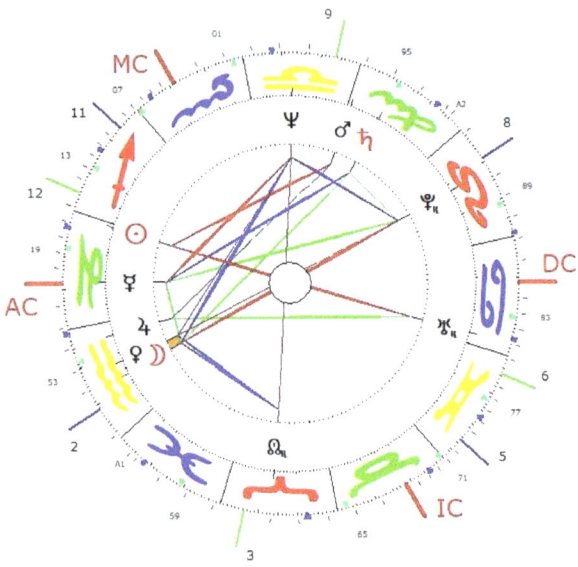

Figure 6 Frieda, 23.12.1949, 0925, Luzern, CH

Even as a child I was already looking for answers to the questions "where do I come from, where am I going and why am I here". I hoped to receive explanations in religious instruction and in the convent school. I observed people, their posture, facial expressions, their verbal expression. An endless search for the meaning of life. Together with the fulfillment of everyday life, this often means excessive demands.

In 1988 I attended a course called The Elements. I was excited! I then began training with Louise and Bruno Huber. The Huber Method is a wonderful tool for understanding difficult things.

Upon entering the 12th house, I was full of anticipation of what the passage through the 12th house will bring me. When the AP was conjunct my Capricorn Sun, I was hit with a tsunami of memories, especially of childhood and adolescence. These memories were real and connected to all the feelings I'd had. Sometimes I saw every detail in front of me and the unanswered questions were there again. Frustration, anger, disappointment alternated with joy, gratitude and trust in what is to come.

As the AP stood midway between the Sun and Mercury (around LP 12), Mercury helped to analyze memories in a more concrete and realistic way. I met people who told me about an experience that had to do with me. I heard about well-kept secrets that brought me clarification.

My horoscope is not consistent. The 'closed' linear figure between the Sun, Mars, Jupiter and Uranus is mostly not seen. For me, this is important, because almost all significant Age Points that shaped me are connected to this figure.

Also, the AP of my Crossing Point axis 2-8 is connected to that linear figure. Now I'm excited to see what new experiences the journey through the 1st house will bring.

5.1.6 Uschi

Uschi describes her 12th house conflicts between freedom and belonging, and between living in South Africa and Germany, and is ready to open up a new chapter in her life..

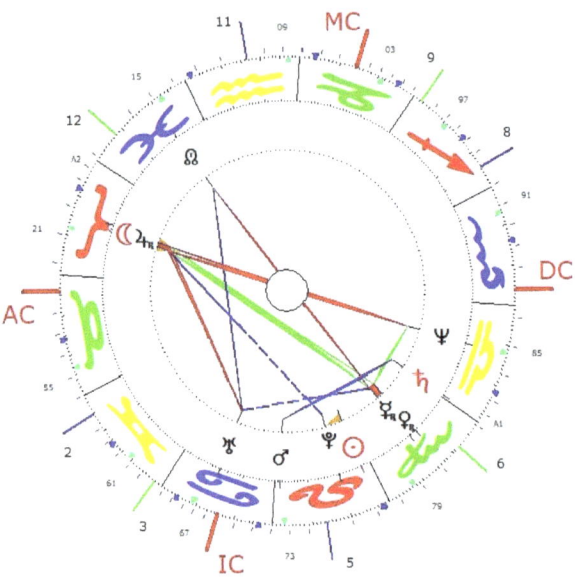

Figure 7 Uschi 20/08/1951 2140, Singen, Germany

Uschi's Background

I lived in South Africa from October 1973 until December 2016 and had a lifelong interest, even passion, for astrology. I did a basic study in Astro-Psychology during 1986 with Maureen Demot at the Institute of Astro-Psychology in Johannesburg. Later I decided to deepen my knowledge of astrology and had the opportunity to study Astrological Psychology with APA in London (online from South Africa) after my children were grown up. I received my diploma in

October 2012 and must say that I have never regretted doing this course and am very grateful for everything I learned. Now and then I do charts for friends and acquaintances and am happy to say that I always get positive feedback.

In December 2016 I moved back to my home country Germany, after separating from my husband.

12th house

My AP entered the 12th house in August 2017. That year was for me a period of new beginnings. It was also quite a stressful time. At times I had that deep feeling of loss which I pushed back which of course is typical for the 12th house. Even though the decision to separate from my husband with whom I had emigrated to South Africa in 1973, came from myself, it was not easy. After all I was married for more than 40 years.

Before 2017: How it all developed

During my marriage I had a deep longing for personal freedom and to have time to explore myself and my own interests, which always took second place. But I was and still am able to look back at my life with a sense of accomplishment and even gratitude because I have 3 wonderful sons and I have mostly good memories of South Africa, its wonderful weather, nature and people.

This is all hard to put into words, which is fitting for the 12th house because it works mostly in the subconscious. My husband was always possessive and demanding, so somehow I expected to come to Germany and feel free and happy. But of course, while part of me surely felt that way I found it difficult to break free from my memories and my past and enjoy my present life. It was also a big risk financially because we were still in divorce negotiations and nothing was settled financially. But my Leo Sun and planets in Aries took over and I took the risk. Looking back, I realize that there is this subtle and deep-seated conflict between my personality as shown by many of my planets in the fire element and the environment (house structure) which has such a strong 12th house with the conjunction of Moon and Jupiter there. Moreover, my Crossing Axis is also 6/12.

When I first got interested in astrology and did my own chart in 1980 I always had a deep down feeling that my 12th house and especially the Moon/Jupiter conjunction in Aries was my most important psychological aspect (my Achilles heel.)

I truly can say that for me there was throughout my life this conflict between my intercepted Aries Moon and its placement in the 12th house which wants me to be impulsive and get things started. But at the same time circumstances have often been a big challenge and have thrown this impulsiveness and openness back in my face. For example, throughout my marriage friends around me admired me very much for my strength and courage and for what I did for family and business but the person who counted most, my husband, never gave me great support or encouragement. This was the main reason for our final breakup which took place when Uranus went over my Moon in 2014/2015, when I had the urge and courage to break free.

2018: Cusp 12, AP opposition Venus in Virgo

In June 2018 the opposition from AP to Venus in Virgo coincided with a breakup with a man I had met, with whom I felt a strong connection. We had a passionate affair for 3 months. Even though he was single, he felt that he needed a separation because in his own words "I am not able to fall in love even though we had such a great time like I had perhaps enjoyed many years ago." He could not connect intimately due to his difficult relationships with women in the past – so I thought – but I was the one who had to pay the price.

2019: AP enters Aries in November, Opposition to Saturn in Libra in December

In October 2019 my mom passed away after being for more than a year in a nursing home. She'd always enjoyed good health, but suddenly had a fall during 2018 and was never her old self again. It was painful to see her suffer like this, lying in bed helpless after she had always led such an active life. One month later my AP went into Aries and in December opposed Saturn in Libra. So perhaps it should have been a time of new beginnings for me.

May 2021: AP at LP 12, Jupiter/Moon conjunction

There was an overall feeling throughout 2021 of frustration. For example I need to do some repairs to my cottage and planned this over 2 years ago. But I have not been able to find the right person or company to do this. It feels like the universe is conspiring against me. I had one company who had signed the offer but always had excuses and never did the job, this happened 2 years ago. Then 7 months ago I found a good artisan who promised he would come in March this year, his health is not so good anymore so he decided a few weeks ago that he cannot do the job. For me, this seems to prove the point that my Aries planets are really not happy in the 12th house and whatever I plan and try and put into action, circumstances (12th house) conspire against me.

What the 12th house means for me

I do believe that especially the AP in a chart has more subtle and long term meanings because for about 6 months I've been feeling restless and unsure of what I want to do with the rest of my life, a feeling of uncertainty and an urge to still do something meaningful, even perhaps make a big change like moving back to South Africa. But this time I will think about it carefully and not be too impulsive. Remember, my Aries planets always want to go into action.

It feels to me like a wave tries to pull me into a new direction, like a glimpse on the horizon beckoning me to new beginnings. At the same time there is a sense of loss, my sons are all leading their own life and my family was for many years the centre of my existence, so I do miss the times when we were all still together. So now finally I am free but freedom by itself is meaningless for me. I am fortunate that I have made good friends here in my neighbourhood and there is even a man who loves me very much but while I like him a lot I also have my reservations. He wants nothing more from life then to enjoy his retirement with me, but I am still full of dreams and plans, even to the point of fulfilling one of my dreams of owning a game lodge in South Africa. I could not do this before because of commitments with family and business.

So perhaps the 12th house lesson is really to sit back and just let things happen, no more high flying plans because after all I am now 70 years old and should learn to let things flow.
I am lucky enough to have a part time job in an advertising agency which part of me really enjoys because I love liaising with people. But I've realised to my surprise that I do not really want this anymore. My boss is happy to have me there and

compares me to a Porsche i.e. a self-starter and says I can still go very far but the point is that I do not really need this. I know that I can do this but I'd rather do astrology, or some other spiritual work more fitting for the 12th house.

The next issue with the 12th house is of course mental and physical health. I always took for granted that I am healthy most of my life but even there I have to realise that my body is aging. I had a bad fall in January this year while I was visiting my one son in South Africa; we were walking in the bush and I fell over a tree stump. Nothing broken but my knee still hurts sometimes. So there is my 6/12th house emphasis of which I have always been very much aware. Physical and mental health are 2 sides of the same coin.

Being now back from a holiday in South Africa I am "digesting" all my memories and still feel very drawn back to that country. This would be a big decision, Regardless of what I decide, I have this feeling that I am facing a door and just have to push it to open up a new chapter in my life. It's really a time where I am looking back at my life trying to find meaning in everything that happened, which I think is typical of the 12th house.

AP will still be in the 12th house until I turn 72 next August. I hope that I have the necessary maturity to make the right decisions before it crosses the AC in Taurus. My astrological studies have often helped me to have clarity on why this or that is happening, but I realize that it is a long learning process and you realize only later what really took place because often things happen subtly and subconsciously. It is like brewing up and developing and needs patience and faith that whatever happens will be OK. For me, the saying is really true, that life can only be lived forward but understood backward. Then one can be prepared and after the 12th house phase of endings there can really be a new beginning, learning from past mistakes. Once I am there I really hope that I will have clarity and wisdom to do that.

5.1.7 Gabrielle

Gabrielle, a German astrological psychologist, describes losing her husband near the 12th house Low Point.

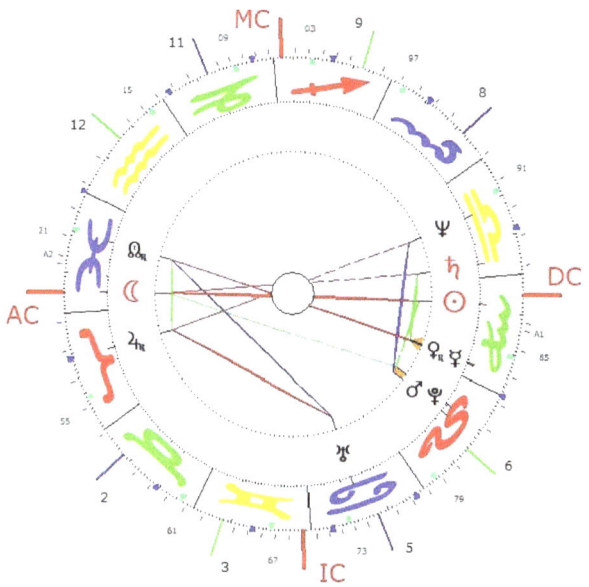

Figure 8 Gabrielle 15/09/1951, 18.45, Telgte (bei Münster), Germany

LP 12 and North Node

I turned 70 last September 15th, going over the North Node and LP 12. My husband had a massive brain haemorrhage on November 22nd. He was in hospital for four weeks, after which I took him home to care for him there. He passed away January the 17th.

I am approaching Crossing Point 2.

I am on my own for the first time in this life. Well, there were a few years before when I lived alone, but during that time we were already lovers…

I am lucky to be quite well off, having a house of my own where we lived together for 43 years.

I also use the solar horoscope and solar age-progression, as in radix AP. In that solar chart my age point was exactly on Uranus the 22nd of November.

And I use the solar-radix-klick. My husband died on the node in conjunction with Moon.

5.1.8 Katharina

Katharina reflects on her experience of the 12th house.

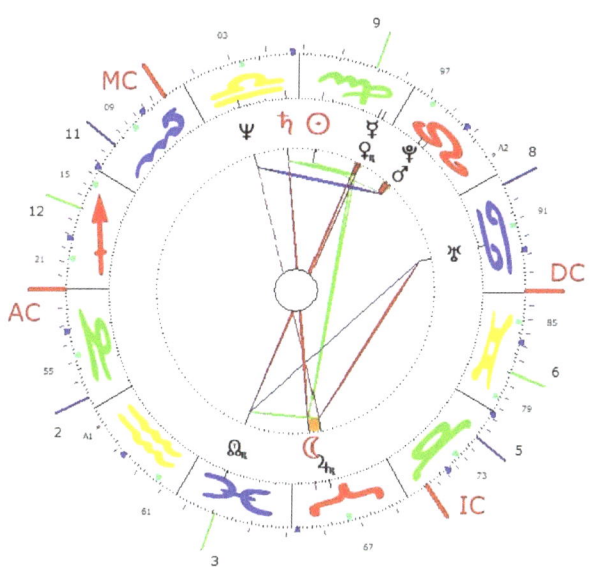

Figure 9 Katharina, 16/09/1951, 1535, London, England

Katharina's Chart

My chart image is a bit like a diabolo. The planets are spread over just 2 quadrants; most of them in the 3rd, 8th and 9th houses.

The sun has just a single faint aspect (towards Mars/Pluto). 6 planets are near the Low Points. 6 planets are in an intercepted signs. The only two planets that are not in some such way "reduced" in their acting to the outside world are Mercury conjunct Venus near cusp 9.

I have no planets in the 12th house or near the AC or DC, so no major conjunctions or oppositions in the 12th house.

AP into 12th house

I took up a pension and stopped working. When I was 36 years old (AP on DC), I had also stopped working because I began to stay at home with my two baby boys. I buy less things, because I'm always thinking that I already possess one of the like.

I attended several courses and learned skills I'd always wanted to learn like glass-manufacturing, bookbinding, calligraphy. I'd like to practise foreign languages (English, French, Spanish) and to study a new one like Georgian (and to travel there)!

I have new insight about life in a relationship: Accept things the way they are. Stop trying to get more understanding. I now see myself more clearly or in a different light: I realise I should do the things that I've always wanted to do, like travelling, painting, meet friends.

LP 12 – Age 70

Travelling (the 12th house is in Sagittarius) without my husband. I attended an English course in Southern England, staying with a host-family. It was great. AP was square Sun around this time.

I'm beginning to think about reducing my collected stuff. As I'm "double-earth" (sun and AC in earth-sign) collecting is easy and enjoyable for me. But giving away or throwing way is hard. I'm fascinated by the idea of living in a "tiny house". (The minimalism of Capricorn is diametrically opposite to the life-theme of being a collector.)

I have come to accept the 'negative' parts of my character, and try to live with them in a way that is not harmful to others.

As I approach the AC, my AC sign Capricorn becomes more meaningful. Its esoteric seed thought[47] has been with me throughout my life. I'm often in a mood of thinking, that I'm not getting what I would like to have or not being able to reach out for what I could get. (Or not allow myself to be happy, in order not to make another person feel jealous.)

---

[47] Seed thought for Capricorn: "Lost am I in light supernal, yet on that light I turn my back." Huber, Louise, *Reflections and Meditations on the Signs of the Zodiac*.

5.1.9 Georgina and Paul

Non-astrologers Georgina and Paul are a retired couple. Georgina knows her time of birth and her responses can be considered against her natal chart. Paul doesn't know his time of birth. His chart is set up as for noon with an unknown time of birth, so his general observations on life in the 1st house can't be referred to specifically. However, the contributions he's made regarding this stage of life are valid and reflect the trend of responses we've received from astrologers and the other non-astrologers whose accounts we've included.

Georgina

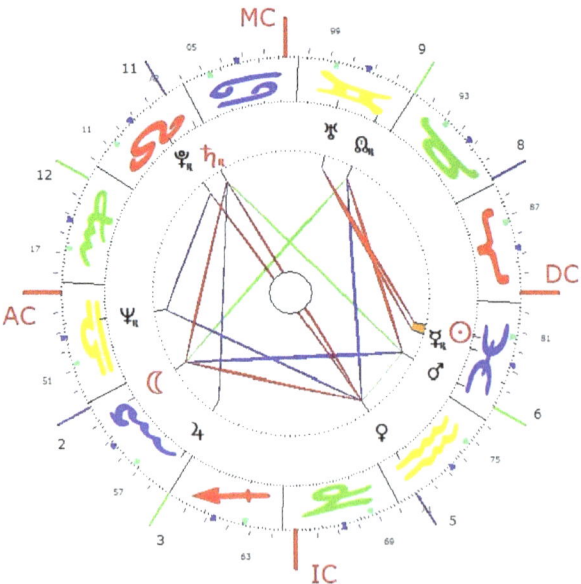

Figure 10 Georgina 10/03/1947, 1910, Leeds, England

When Georgina's AP was on LP 12 her 104 year old mum died, two days after Georgina's 70th birthday. She'd been her mum's carer for some time, since her mum moved to live with them. Georgina has mixed feelings about losing her mum, as caring took up much of her time and her life.

AP returned to the 1st house in 2019, moving towards Neptune, the only planet there. Between ages 72-73, Georgina discovered a lump in her breast and underwent surgery for a lumpectomy and subsequent treatment. This was particularly concerning as she'd recovered from a full mastectomy in 1995. Her health came under more pressure during this period while AP was under the influence of Neptune; she had a TIA episode (mini stroke), resulting in her being prescribed statins. She also became more vigilant about her health.

In 2020, she started to write a daily lockdown diary of what life was like as the country closed down, and of what she and Paul did, intending it to be a historic record and account for her grandchildren.

Georgina and Paul

Both Georgina & Paul said that with AP in 1st house they were and are doing more of what they want to. Reviewing their lives post-Covid they've agreed that family and health comes first. Both noted they are becoming more insular and family-oriented.

With regard to maintaining old friendships, Georgina is good at this, Paul is not and says he doesn't feel the need. Georgina needs a social life so keeps the friendships going. Both are more selective about friendships and they are comfortable as a couple. Paul says they value what they have together and that he is more conscious of their mortality.

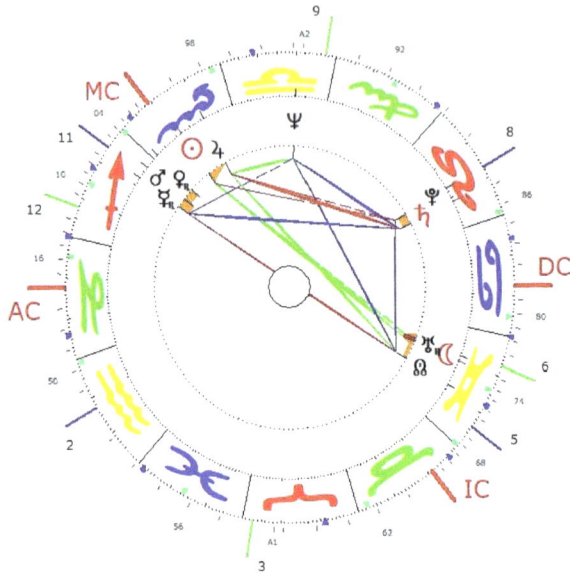

Figure 11 Paul 11/11/1946,1200, Wakefield, England

Georgina, having worked as a special needs teacher, doesn't want targets or stress in her life, preferring to be easy in what she does. She doesn't want to do lots of cooking or entertaining these days, and goes for easy life wherever possible. She's good at researching things thoroughly, like new places they might go to, and always checks these out before they go, so she knows about the place. She says she's enquiring and likes doing the research.

Both of them have had cancer scares in the past few years and they're aware of the implications of this, so aim to enjoy and value life in the 1st house, spending time and sharing holidays with family and grandchildren.

Both reflected on their move from Durham to Yorkshire when in the 7th house, saying that when they moved away from Durham they tried to make new friends, but now don't feel the need to, suggesting echoes across the chart from houses 1/7 and I/You sides of chart – a correlation between experiences and needs of 34/36 years ago and now, back in the 1st house.

5.1.10 Elly

Elly's journey through the 12th house included the death of her partner, Richard Llewellyn, co-founder of the English Huber School.

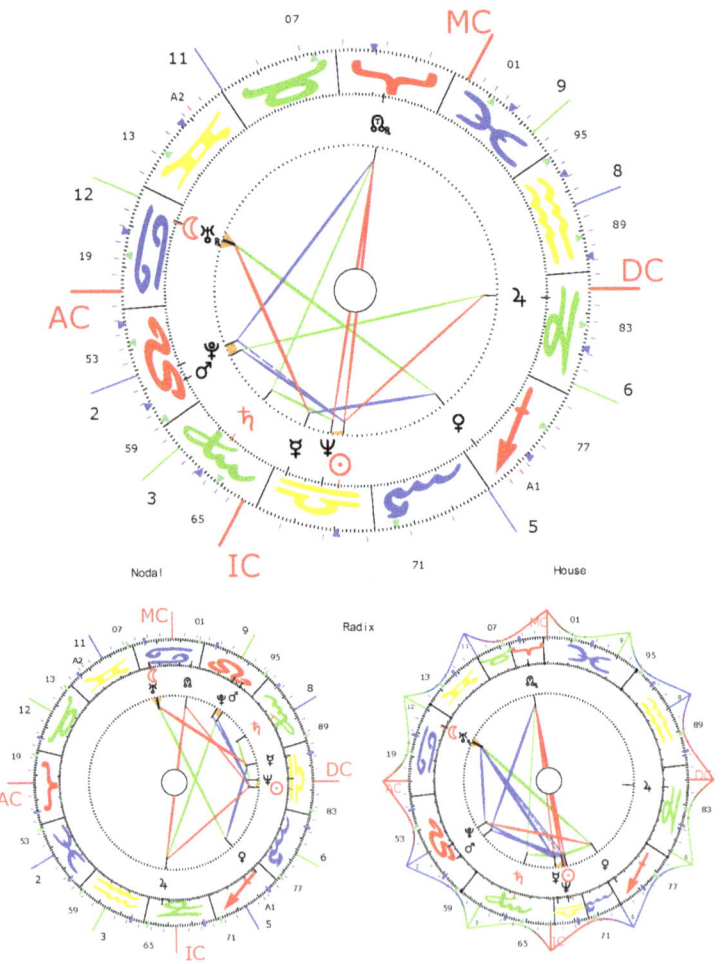

Figure 12 Elly, 13/10/1949, 2330, Liverpool, England

I have over the years viewed my life's journey as chapters in a book and at this present time I have started a new one. As in a book, people who were in previous chapters continue in my story and memories and experience build and bind the book together.

12th House

I am starting with my journey through the 12th house as I have a close Moon/Uranus conjunction roughly 5° into this house, in the sign of Cancer. This conjunction is strong by house but weak by sign. Moon/Uranus has been a great influence in my life and my age at this conjunction was 67. Although I can't say that I noticed anything much different when my AP reached Moon/Uranus, I know that I began to reflect about my life and the future.

All through Cancer, for the next 5 years up to the AC, partner Richard and I were joining a party of Normandy Veterans going to Normandy each year to commemorate D-Day and the Normandy Landings. Even though I was long since retired as an Operating Theatre Sister, I still had a great feeling of responsibility in a quiet way to make sure that everybody was all right.

Richard's Death 09/02/2021

My natal chart. AP opposition Jupiter in the stress area of the 6th house, semisextile to Mars/Pluto in the 2nd house in Leo.

Nodal chart. AP opposition Sun/Neptune conjunction in Libra, 6th house and sextile to Mars/Pluto in Leo on the 8th house.

House chart. AP opposition Jupiter in the 6th house but Jupiter is unaspected and therefore a free agent to go where it wants. I have to confess that after Richard's death I had a strong sense of freedom to have my life to myself again.

In the 10 days before Richard's death I automatically took control of the situation that was unfolding at home – Mars/Pluto in the node chart. I was joined by my two daughters and Richard's daughter as we all looked after him in his final days. There was a great deal of Sun/Neptune love and peace between us and we formed a strong bond.

At this time with opposition Jupiter in my Natal chart and opposition unaspected Jupiter in my House chart I felt a compelling energy to embark on a new chapter and build my life again. I feel a bit guilty saying this, but Richard and I were together for just over 25 years and I know that he wanted me to be happy.

I think of my unaspected Jupiter in the House chart as a freelance journalist in my life that discovers new experiences and situations. I am singing in choirs, gone back to tap dancing and learning to play Mahjong. Jupiter likes to be part of a group and expand my horizons.

This Libran, being an air sign, is not outwardly emotional, but this doesn't mean that I don't have emotions or empathy with people and situations, it's just that sometimes I have to think about how I feel. This is a 1st ray Moon/Uranus and it has always been the same for all my life.

I have done a lot of reflection about myself and relationships. Perhaps it began with my AP reaching Moon/Uranus but only came to light in my head now that I am on my own.

Although I sing in choirs, join other groups and have friends, I don't now need or want another close relationship. I feel that over the years I have given too much of myself away. This is me reflecting on the relationships and on what I need for myself and my place in the world.

Passing the AC

My age is now 72 I have just passed the AC in Cancer and I suspect this has also been a time of reflection and 1st house energy to move forward. The Cancer esoteric seed thought is "I build a Lighted House and therein dwell." By accepting myself as a whole being who is positive about life I hope that others can also make steps forward when life seems to drag them back.

The Libra esoteric seed thought also ties in with this. "I Choose the way which leads between the two great lines of force." Uranus is the esoteric ruler of Libra and I have read that it is the pacesetter and progressive in decisions. Surely my opposition to Sun/Neptune in Libra in my nodal chart would have an influence on me.

I have the same birth date as Mrs Thatcher and "This Lady is not for turning" either. I will leave you all to look at my chart and decide which part of my chart has the most influence on this statement.

5.1.11 Trish

Trish's story was a response to the request for supplementary input on the 36-year echo effect

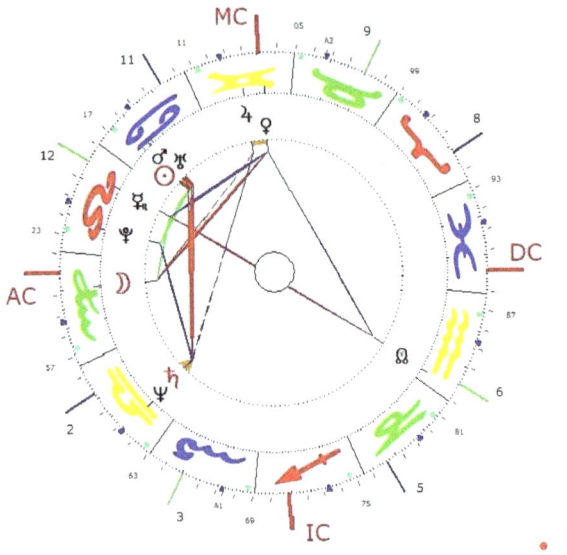

Figure 13 Trish, 15.07.1953, 0920, Nakuru, Kenya

I would like to focus on the 2nd – 8th house LP opposition (ages 9¾, 45¾), as these were particularly profound points in my life. LP 2 was preceded by my Neptune/Saturn conjunction making strongly pronounced square aspects to my 11th house Sun/Mars/Uranus stellium. This indicates a tension I experienced between my father (Sun) and mother (Saturn) starting at roughly age 8½. My awareness of this (underpinned by my father's affair) continued to heighten through these later childhood years, culminating in their separation when I was nearly 12, on the cusp of the 3rd house.

At this time I left Kenya on a ship with my mother and brother to come to relatives in the suburbs of Surrey, England. My mother had to find a place for us to rent, while my father and new wife-to-be, stayed in Kenya living in a large house and garden which came with his job. It was a very traumatic time: total life change, change of environment, climate, starting a new secondary school, everything. The association of the 2nd house with loss and low self-esteem is very accurate!

But I think it precipitated a search in me for meaning and purpose, stimulated by the 11th house planets. The 11th house is characterized in part by seeking the source of human suffering. My search was personal, broadening out to a greater transpersonal level. I became interested in my teens in all the 'isms' – Buddhism, Communism, and had an early interest in astrology, together with human origins – I studied archaeology and anthropology at university.

Moving forward 36 years to my 8th house, this was a period of an intense flowering. It was as if everything experienced so far culminated here. My spiritual interests were expansive, triggered by the opposition to Neptune in the 2nd house. I was fascinated by spiritual healing, past lives, reincarnation, astrology, to an almost obsessive level (8th house). As I reached the LP in all this exploration, I found an advert for Huber Astrology, and felt this was what I needed. A need to focus my interests and become more grounded as I approached the sign change to Taurus, and this astrology with its deeply spiritual underpinning was right.

And so it was that I began to study for the Foundation Course Certificate in 1998, age 45, and continuing shortly after to study the API Diploma, age 46. This was all around the time approaching the LP and shortly thereafter.

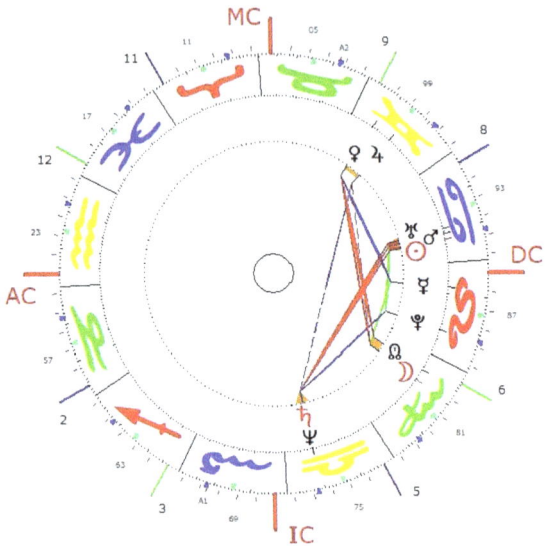

Figure 14 Trish Nodal chart

Ever since it has been an immensely important part of my life, encompassing all of my interests. Through examining my Nodal (past life) chart, I have come to understand the karmic reasons for my experiences. This chart is notable by its complete contrast to my Natal chart. The latter is very I-sided, the Nodal is very You-sided. It is about teaching me to loosen my ties of dependence on others and partnership (my Sun stellium is in the 7th house of partnership) and develop greater autonomy. The Hubers write at some length about this displacement: "People with the Sun in the 7th Moon Node house have laid up a rich store of experience where partnership is concerned… In several lives it was certainly the mainspring of her life to find a partner, to devote herself to others, and to set aside her own development". But with a drastic displacement to the other side of the chart, "development is likely to be hurried on by some profoundly disturbing experience. Only in this way can ingrained habits be overcome. The native is liable to suffer a trauma in early childhood"[48]. But also that such a drastic displacement is hard to cope with in a single life, and may require several lives for its accomplishment[49].

Well, I do believe that I am not emotionally or intellectually dependent on others. As Liz Greene points out: "in the end the thing which is sought is inner integration… inner wholeness rather than dependency upon another person for the centre of one's psychic life"[50].

I find I am forever grateful for this gift of understanding and making sense of my life that the Hubers have given me, and the English Huber School for facilitating it.

---

[48] Bruno & Louise Huber, *Moon Node Astrology*, HopeWell 2005, pp177-8.
[49] Ibid, p176
[50] Greene, Liz, Saturn: *A New Look at an Old Devil*, p.64

5.2 Stories from the 1st House

Those responding from the 1st house are generally in the age range 72-78, well into their second time around the Life Clock.

    5.2.1 Suzanne

    5.2.2 Klaudia

    5.2.3 Monica

    5.2.4 John

    5.2.5 Annie

    5.2.6 Lily

    5.2.7 Hermann

    5.2.8 Will

    5.2.9 Peter

5.2.1 Suzanne

Suzanne reflects on transformative experiences and insights she's had moving between the Low Points of the 12th and 1st houses.

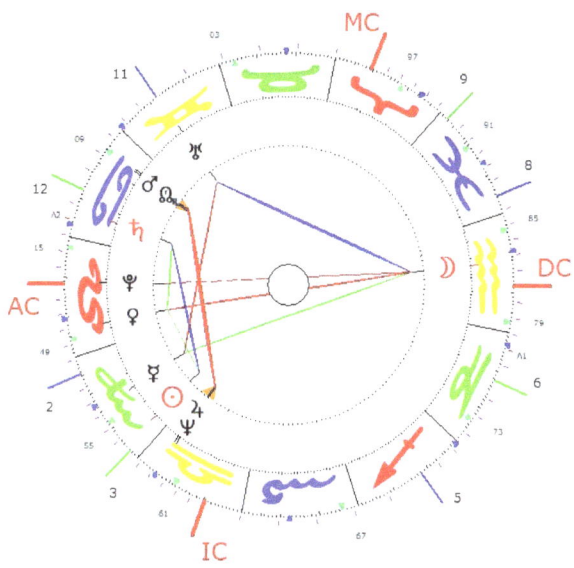

Figure 15 Suzanne, 19/09/1945, 0230, Tadcaster, England

12th house LP, Saturn and Pluto

I knew exactly where I wanted to be on my 70th birthday. Vienna, at the opera.

I'd already done a fair amount of travelling that year, visiting my family in Houston, Texas, to meet my new grandson for the first time, and whilst there taking a short trip to New Orleans. I'd been to the Scottish Highlands, to Normandy, and with the prospect of a tour of European countries in our campervan to look forward to, it didn't feel quite the 12th house LP year I'd expected. Or was it? The LP is not necessarily quiet. Louise Huber often said that at the LP we are closer to the soul's purpose, and I'd learned from previous LPs that there can be plenty going on at an inner level.

The Hubers[51] suggest that the Low Point begins to take effect up to 8 months before the Age Point's exact transit, and that prior to LP 12 the individual may be adjusting to retirement and withdrawing from the outer world and into him or herself. I felt busy and stimulated during this period, with the greater and broader variety of life experiences I had as I travelled, saw new places and met different people. These experiences and encounters offered fresh insights on life, as some of them brought me face to face with my own expectations, attitudes and values.

Perhaps the real LP moment for me was the day before my 70th birthday, on a metro train in Vienna. The doors had closed but the train didn't start. A large number of armed police appeared on the platform, boarded the train and began a forensic search of every compartment while passengers sat frozen in a still, tense hush. An announcement was made, in German, about suspected terrorism and several heavily armed officers, one with a taser on his belt, walked slowly through the train, guns ready, as they scanned the overhead coat racks and under the seats. I caught the eye of a woman sitting across the gangway; she looked as scared as I felt. I'd sussed out that the safest place to be, should any shooting break out, was under the

---

[51] Huber, Bruno & Louise, *Life Clock*, HopeWell

seat and I seriously considered I might not see my 70th birthday the next day.

The police found nothing, the doors were opened and husband, daughter and I got off the train and hurried to the exit. I was shaken and felt as though I'd been jolted in one swift instant from my comfort zone to a raw dark place, where all I could do was exist in the moment. With relief and thanks, I realised I would, after all, see my 70th birthday and get to the opera next day. I'd survived.

My Age Point's journey through the 12th house had already been conjunct Saturn at age 67, when my family and first grandchild left the UK to start a new life in Houston, Texas. Saturn is in the 12th house in both my natal and node charts. The second intersection of natal and nodal age points – the crossing point – at age 68, is also in the 12th house, on the Existence axis. The Hubers speak of the significance of the axis where the intersection points occur; unfinished business is suggested in this area of life, more work to be done along the theme of the house and/or planet involved, plus a familiarity with the meaning and essence of the planet and house involved.

My 12th house LP sits midway between two strong planets – Saturn and Pluto on the AC. So what was going on? Was this some kind of multiple whammy? Preparation for the next stage of the journey around my chart? I think it was. I was meeting strong planets head-on in the house which is traditionally tagged as an area of retreat into old age, a time of stepping back. But I felt there was a message of "there's more work to do" as a theme of existence, of being here and, most importantly, of why am I here, has emerged as I've considered my experiences.

Pluto on AC and survival

At age 72, with Pluto on the AC greeting me as my AP entered the 1st house for the second time in September, I had another powerful personal brush with survival, that of my family. In late August our visiting family and grandchildren returned home to Houston a day ahead of the arrival of Hurricane Harvey. The hurricane, which had been moving slowly across the Gulf of Mexico before making landfall on the Texas coast, brought a period of intensely prolonged rainfall and extensive flooding. It had a major impact on the lives and safety of many people, our family included.

This coincided with a planned campervan tour in Europe. Unable to do anything except stay in touch to support the family, we spent the first day of our holiday on a campsite in Ghent, on the phone and watching live internet coverage of Houston's flooding. The theme of survival kicked in again as we learned the family had packed essentials for evacuation of their home as the waters rose. I was trapped in moments of darkness, experiencing deep fears for their safety. They were lucky. The floods stopped short of their house, leaving them isolated but safe. With my AC Pluto opposite the Moon, my emotions were intense.

This brings echoes of something else, not consciously remembered. Soon after my birth, 72 years previously, I'd contracted an infection which resulted in a large abscess forming under an armpit. At three weeks old I was operated on and the fluid drained. I have a scar, the only physical evidence of this event, and I was separated from my mother who feared I might not survive. She visited me, but this was long before the days of parents staying by a child's bedside in hospital; it was almost two months before I was able to return home. What I experienced in Ghent felt like another manifestation of the survival theme, laced with anxiety of conscious separation from my family.

I had no expectations of what entering the 1st house as an adult would be like. I knew from studying age progression that there could be new awakenings and realisations, and perhaps a reconnection with my inner child. There certainly is, as I continue to enjoy interactions, fun and games with my grandchildren. What a huge bonus and a lot of joy this brings to being in the 1st house again! I was also aware that once in this house, I would come under the influence of Venus, the only planet there. While my AP has been in this house, transiting Pluto has been joined by transiting Saturn. Both have opposed natal Saturn, echoing my earlier brush with these two strong planets at LP 12 and highlighting the "work in progress" effect of my 12th house Saturn in both natal and node charts on the Existence axis.

Moon Node Chart and Uranus

The message of "there's more work to do", and my question of why I'm here was reinforced by the Moon Node AP's conjunction with Uranus in the 1st house in my Nodal chart. Uranus, strong by sign and strongly placed on 11th cusp in my natal chart, is part of the Dominant Learning triangle connected to Moon and Mercury in both charts. With Mercury involved, I've talked, taught, counselled and written about astrology for the past 34 years. With the focus on Uranus – the planet associated with astrology – I began researching and writing about it again, but from a senior years perspective.

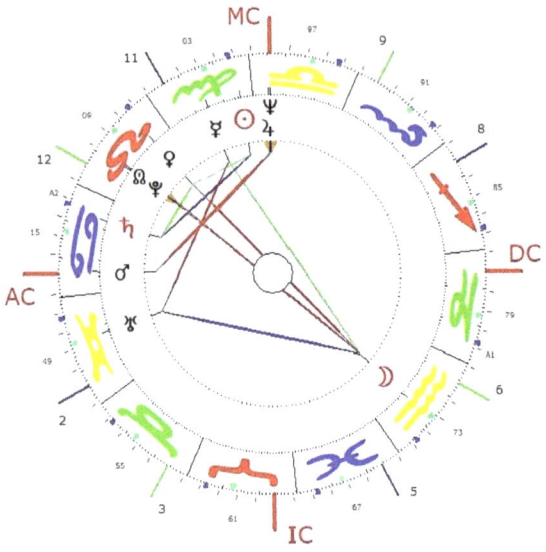

Figure 16 Suzanne Nodal chart

Louise Huber once told me to look at my Moon Node chart to see what was going on underneath, at an inner level. This connection with Uranus appears to be part of the "work to be done".

In *Life Clock* the Hubers write, "When we reach the AC at age 72, we have often entered the AC sign some years before". They suggest that when this happens, it is relatively easy to identify with the qualities of this sign because they have already become part of our inner self. The esoteric seed thoughts for each sign can indicate the direction of our goals, the meaning of our lives and what attitudes and qualities we should seek to develop as we mature. I go along with that. I now have much more insight of the esoteric meaning of Leo, my AC sign – "I am That and That am I." Comfortable with myself and who I am, I'm willingly researching life after 70. It's where I am now and what's gone before, good or bad, has formed and shaped me and brought me to this place. Words of songs from a couple of musicals come to mind and resonate with me: "I am what I am" from *La Cage aux Folles*, and "This is me" from *The Greatest Showman.*

Venus-Moon, changing relationships

With AP conjunct 1st house Venus opposite Moon, both on the 1/7 Encounter axis, I've been evaluating myself and my relationships, contacts and friendships – their value, importance and permanence. I've examined the depth, richness and quality of my interactions with others, and have realised that now I'm back in the 1st house I'm far more selective and discriminating about who I choose to spend time with. Venus at the apex of the Ear/Eye figure connects with and awakens all three Ego planets of body (Saturn), feelings (Moon) and mind (Sun), making me acknowledge that I'm no longer willing to waste time and energy on unfulfilling relationships. I'm far more comfortable these days being straight, truthful and outspoken. Some friendships have been tested, failed and discarded. One in particular, which originated over forty years ago and should have been terminated there and then re-emerged, triggering issues which were not cleared when my AP was in the 7th house, crossing LP 7 and aspecting Venus, Pluto and Sun. There is an uncanny and interesting "36 years echo" at work here and I've welcomed the opportunity to work with it and move on.

Long standing friendships have been rekindled and new friends made; these days I'm now more perceptive and discriminating in who I can trust and who I can't. Learning to trust, listen to and act on my intuition has been a hard-learned "second time around" 1st house and 1st quadrant lesson.

Some of my 1st house experiences and insights happened during the extended period of lockdowns in the first two years of the Coronavirus pandemic. As life slowed down there was time to focus on what was really important, like being more closely in touch with nature, watching birds and insects close up, as I did when a child. Meeting with Venus head on here I also became more focussed on my physical and mental health.

As a child, my AP was conjunct Venus when I started dance lessons and began performing on stage in dancing school shows. My nerves about this at age 4 were overcome by the excitement of dressing up in stage costumes, wearing rouge and lipstick and having my hair curled. This time around, with hairdressers closed, I let my hair grow. My image has changed as I've revisited the look and style I had 30 years ago. This is the external expression of how I feel, renewed both inside and out. In a Pluto-like way, I've sorted and cleaned out what was no longer relevant. I have a stronger sense of self and more self-confidence as I embrace and accept being in my mature years.

LP 1

The 1st house LP experience has at times been challenging, difficult, dark and disappointing because of Covid restrictions. Friends, family and people I'd cared about have died, but this was offset by the high point of getting together with my family and grandchildren after 18 months of separation. The LP has been a time of quiet stasis and introspection and now I'm moving on. My AP is in the mutable zone and has moved into Virgo with the practicality and grounding this sign offers. As I move towards the 2nd house I've already begun evaluating possessions and parting with things no longer relevant, or that I no longer want or need. When my AP gets there, I will come under the influence of Sun and Mercury, potential partners in this stage of the journey for information gathering and writing about astrological psychology.

On reflection, Pluto on the AC has been calling the shots for some time. I've had significant, transformative experiences and insights. I've made personal and psychological changes to myself and my outlook over the past 6 years, and I've questioned what my role, if any, is meant to be – or if I even need a "role". Pluto, for me, has always been about renewal and regeneration, where what is of importance is retained while the old and outdated is jettisoned in favour of opening up space for the new. I'm ready to grow into that space.

5.2.2 Klaudia

Klaudia reflects on her eventful early childhood and her experience moving from the 12th house LP and into the 1st house, in search of a spiritual home

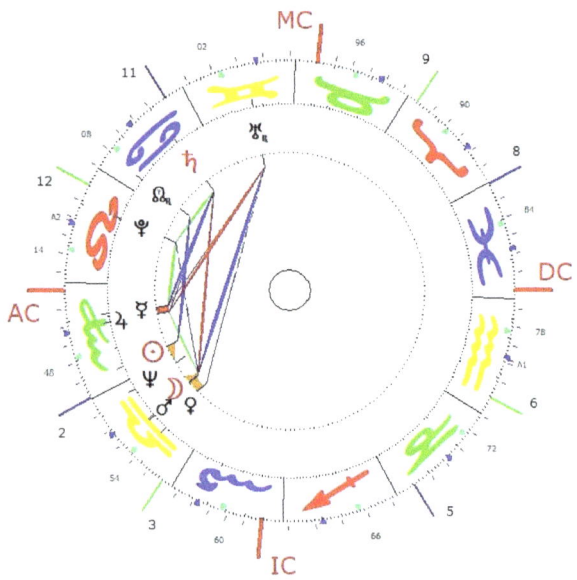

Figure 17 Klaudia 19/09/1944, 0237, Leoben, Austria

The first time around

Through my mother's stories I am well aware of the first six years of my life; they have accompanied me throughout my life.

My parents, a civil engineer (and mountaineer during the war) from Berlin and a secretary from Leoben met in Styria, Austria in 1942. They both loved the high mountains. In 1944 I was born. My father was a soldier back in Tyrol, and my mother lived with her mother in Styria.

My father deserted in March 1945 and came back to us, hiding in the nearby forest. One day a small group of Russian soldiers came to my grandmother's house, looking for German soldiers. The leader said: "Where there's a child, there's a man," pointing a gun at me on my mother's arm. A young woman from Ukraine, who was living and working at my grandmother's farm as an alternative war service at the time, translated my mother's words saying that my father had not yet returned. She saved me and my mother, and also my father's life.

In May 1945 World War II came to an end, and the British Allies occupied and administered Styria, granting my father a job as an interpreter at the British base because of his good knowledge of English. A modest and mostly quiet life began with my father, mother and grandmother. Between 1947 and 1948 (LP 1) the horizon of my life as an only child broadened when I entered the Leoben ballet school. Mrs. Roberti, a ballerina, was my first teacher. That meant 'group experience', but beyond that, bodywork with French ballet language and classical music. There were stage performances, also for the little ones. In 1949 (AP cj Sun) I performed solo for the first time, a wonderful experience. The ballet hall became a second home for me. With physical discipline and diligence one obtains beauty, harmony and a healthy ego.

Yet, that time would literally end overnight. The British occupation of Styria had ended and Austria had become a free country again, making my father a German foreigner. As a consequence, we left Styria in February 1950 to start a new life in Berlin, a job-related move. We temporarily lived with my paternal grandparents in the centre of Berlin, opposite the large natural history museum, where my grandfather helped rebuild the inventory. I found a good friend in the house next door. Together we roamed the large exhibition halls, with my grandfather telling us all kinds of interesting stories. Soon my father found an apartment for us, so we moved to the old Jewish quarter of Grunewald with beautiful old villas and a lot of forest. There were shelled houses everywhere, overgrown by grass and flowers. My paternal grandmother took me under her wing and explained to me that my Styrian dialect was not well understood there. So I learned the high German language and many interesting things in life to prepare for my upcoming school education.

The second time around, beginning in the 12th house

In May 2012, 12th house/ Leo, I had an accident resulting in a splinter fracture in my shin/fibula. This was supported by titanium rod/wire and removed again in 2013/2014 (age 70). An accident happens suddenly, in seconds, while the aftereffects last for years. A great reflection was about to begin. Why? How had life been before, how will it be afterwards? In the 12th house one experiences the finiteness of life on earth. My esoteric studies with Gunda Scholdt were interrupted and could not be continued in the same format.

1-2 years later, the group had changed, new members had joined and everything felt unfamiliar. My Huber education returned. Koch houses instead of equal houses, more focus on Bruno's aspect pictures instead of just looking at individual aspects. But both systems hold many treasures and the study of astrology never ends.

Actually, one does not like to leave the sign Leo. Not until late in life in the 12th house it was my subject. In the beginning of my astrological studies I didn't want to believe that the AC was at 2nd degree of Virgo. I felt like I was still in Leo. Elke Gut, AC 0° Virgo, opened my eyes with her biographical experience.

In 2014 (LP 12) a tremendous power of thought came into play, I started planning a more adequate living situation for life in elderly age. No more second floor, in case of walking insecurities. The small house, formerly my husband's office, was remodelled and renovated. A bright, sunny work/living room was created for reading, writing and special conversation and two very quiet bedrooms. A partial move took place in 2016. Thanks to lots of excellent rehabilitation and physiotherapy after breaking my leg, I have a good daily exercise programme which gives me the strength to do physical work again. But still, you get older physically.

There are other gifts: "the inner doctor", ways to heal yourself and the rich knowledge about the healing power of plants that I learned from my maternal grandmother. After a short study of Dr. Reinhard Witt's work we transformed our garden into a natural garden. More space for wild flowers, insects and birds (2017/18), a holistic approach.

Each day begins with the Great Invocation, written down in the "blue books" by Alice A. Bailey, joining the worldwide group. One step further on the spiral of life? I hope so.

I leave the small house when one of the daughters with their respective partners and the grandchildren announce a visit. Then it's a children's house with a tent in the attic where all my old childhood toys and books are stored. I like sharing them.

Since 2020 the pandemic has severely restricted social life. But at the end of September 2020 (LP 1) another granddaughter was born. She will be at home on two continents because her father has Spanish and American roots. She is learning two languages at the same time, English and German.

5.2.3 Monica

Monica describes a time of reduced horizons after passing the 12th house Low Point.

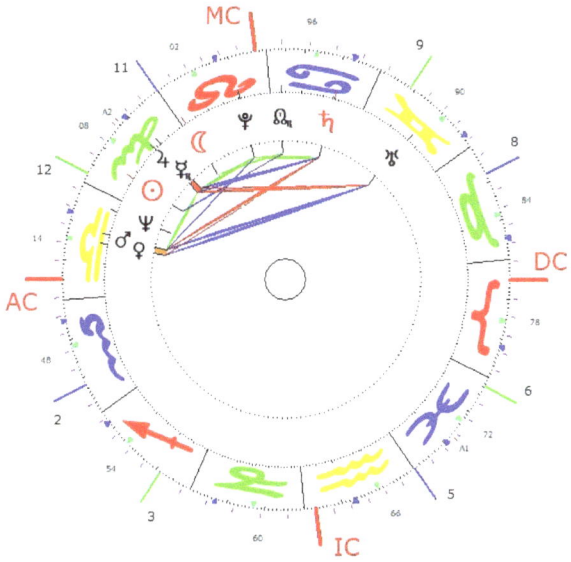

Figure 18 Monica, 15/09/1944, 0955, Leipzig, Germany

LP 12 / Crossing Point

The most significant event since LP 12/Crossing Point was the onset of my husband's serious Parkinson's Disease. Because of this it became more and more difficult to spend time with him outside of our house. Increasingly, I had to do everything for him, because he could not move himself. He began being in permanent need of nursing care, which I undertook myself. I had to be very strong and lead him like a child. My mother-qualities were much in demand.

For the past 4 years I have been living in isolation with my husband. Now he is also demented. Because of the coronavirus-crisis we have been alone together for the past 2 years.

The Venus/Mars conjunction stands on LP 12, and these tools have been necessary for both of us.

AC and the 1st house

Libra is the sign on my AC. I valued this throughout my life until the age of 72. Since then my Moon Node chart with AC in Cancer has become more and more important for me. Now I think I'm living my Moon Node chart and only a little my radix chart.

In the 1st house, when my AP changed from Libra into Scorpio my life became more difficult.

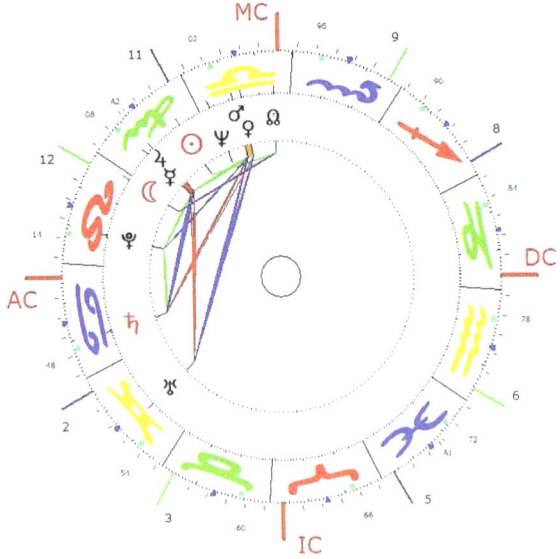

Figure 19 Monica Nodal Chart

The Moon Node chart has Saturn near LP 1. I now have a narrowed horizon. More and more I'd like to be alone. Note that my Moon Node chart is situated completely on the left-hand side.

My AP is now at the end of the 1st house. I'm not extroverted, but more and more introverted. I'm increasingly living my Moon Node chart with its AC in Cancer. My mother-qualities are very much demanded by my environment. My "You"-interests will wane and my "Me"-interests will grow more and more. Also, I must increasingly live the quality (Libra) of the AC of my radix chart. Despite all this, I don't suffer and feel good.

5.2.4 John

As he encounters the AC, John creates a new identity, a new beginning - combining his interests in astrology, psychology and spirituality.

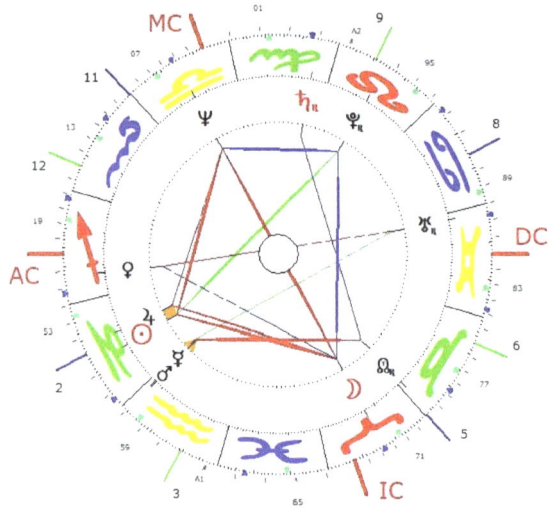

Figure 20 John, 07/01/1949, 0532, Huntingdon, PA, US

I was third born child to a 42-year-old mother. I was born healthy but had acute breathing problems in infancy (first-3 months) due to an enlarged thymus gland. I had radiation treatment to reduce its size as it was obstructing breathing.

Correlation: I am oversensitive to feelings of suffocation from hostile environmental factors and have many allergies; and need to protect myself from environmental harmful effects. Still do. One breathing exercise in yoga makes me feel like I am suffocating. I think it is in my muscle memory that I am afraid to suffocate. In addition, I think since Venus rules my 6th house, that a chart rectification may be in order with Venus closer to the AC because it happened with the autoimmune response so young.

36 years ago

36 years ago, I was going to graduate school and in an internship on an alcoholic detoxification unit with Veterans at a federal hospital. I had to evaluate their commitment to treatment programs for recovery. At that time, I had strong angry and negative feelings (countertransference) when patients would lie to me and not follow through with their treatment. It was a carry-over from my relationship with my alcoholic father who also lied to me about his life. This was June 1985 when the AP was crossing my DC, sextile to natal Moon, sextile Pluto, trine Neptune in 10th house, quincunx to Sun. Correlations where I had to examine myself not to let my ego issues interfere with treatment of sick people. I still have the awareness of not letting my ego get in the way as I have to watch out for my own biases intruding on my helping clients.

LP 12 – Family time, dreams

The LP was conjunct in September 2018 when Judy and I were visiting with my daughter's family in Sardinia. We were enjoying my second granddaughter, 8 months old. We went to the beach and had a relatively quiet time. I remember recording my dreams at that time. Because I had energy to introspect, I found myself revisiting some of the dream shadow images that I had been aware of within myself. That dark side. Where the self-beckons you to want to act out inappropriate behaviors based on seductive images. Of course, being aware of my dreams, I was not, because of ethical principles, acting on any of this. When shadow energies are brought to consciousness, one is aware of the decisions that one could make that would be a violation of ethical values. Whenever these kinds of negative images happened in the dream world, you do not fall prey to projection as much.

When AP was just beyond LP 12, I had a birthday party at home in which my son from Russia and my daughter from Italy and her family came to visit. It was a significant reunion. During that week I took a break from psychotherapy. I had to drive Miranda and family to New York City to JFK airport. I had to break down the trip because I discovered I could not tolerate New York traffic jams.

My shadow: Donald J. Trump and implications of evil leadership:

On 7/3/2019 my obsession (Scorpio on the 12th house cusp) with the negative personality of Donald J. Trump was coming up because Trump wanted to be re-elected. (AP at 10 deg 53' semi-sextile to Jupiter stressed before 2nd house). I had written some articles about him on a blog[52]. These were especially revealing about his personality. He was the type of man who would abandon all rationality and allow himself to be swallowed up by the collective consciousness of the nation. He is ego-ridden and malicious to those who threaten or oppose him. There seemed to be some sort of spiritual battle going on, which was reflected in my dreams. Fortunately Trump's handling of Covid revealed his weakness as a narcissistic leader who failed to competently address the pandemic. The American economy suffered and he was not re-elected.

---

[52] See e.g. https://astrologicalpsychology.org/donald-j-trump/

New Identity at the AC – Astrology and Psychology:

By August 2020 my AP was stressed just before the AC in Sagittarius. (AP was trine Pluto, Moon and sextile Neptune which was my ambivalence rectangle with quincunx being stimulated; Moon Node AP was conjunct 5th house Node square to Mercury/ Mars in 2nd house) I had invested in my own website[53] and it was a shake and break moment of making public my marriage of Psychology and Astrology through synthesizing both. Up to that time I had kept Astrology out of my professional life as a psychotherapist. I compartmentalized astrology out of my discourses on personality in my psychotherapy practice. But now with the website, I blended the two into one. On 7/5/2020 I had the following dream:

> "Two became one. I was taken into a Cave by a woman astrology teacher named Jennifer Gehl for a lesson. There were cows (a symbol of docility?) inside. The lesson was for me to realize 'two becomes one'. Then after that you have a new identity. Then, third, you act as one person in the world."

My new identity was formed. The teacher told me, 'You now act as one person in the world". In dream interpretation, according to Jung, the way to heal a split of polarity and conflict within yourself is by producing a new attitude (through the non-conscious transcendent function). The Self produces a new symbol, which neutralizes the opposites that form the conflict and makes them one. A split within me, in which I compartmentalized astrology and psychology as two separate

---

[53] https://asklepiosconnection.com/

disciplines, was now integrated and represented in the real world as a website, with an address. This process had been a special healing experience for me. (A transit of Saturn with my natal Sun was also happening at the same time.)

Sagittarius insights:

As the AP progressed into approaching the cusp of the first house, I resolved to, as the Sagittarius AC prescribed, strive to move toward and adhere to a spiritual path in which I would transcend beyond the ego somewhat like a Buddhist. "See the goal. I reach the goal and see another."

"9/20/2020, I had the dream of being dropped out of the sky into water (see dream image). Coming from deep underwater, I surfaced to see in the sky the Sagittarius arrow. Judy who was with me in the water saw it too. I quickly turned and swam to a house on the shore. Judy was crying because I was so excited, I kicked her when I swam toward shore. I apologized saying I was too eager to tell my dad what I saw in the sky."

Figure 21 John's dream image

When I thought about this image in the dream, I discovered it is Buddhism that captures my spiritual belief more accurately than some aspects of Christianity. Especially, in the way one perceives mystical experience through dreams, the concept of Karma and the afterlife. I believe I am bringing treasures from the deep unconscious to the surface and becoming receptive to healing energy. I felt so much hope with this dream and it renewed my faith in the Divine guidance from the universe. In the dream, I wanted to show my dad because he had no faith in the Divine and saw man as an animal.

Up to the election of November 2020: it seemed like a very important historical election coming up and a lot was at stake. Other matters important to us which we examined at the time in the light of impending critical times, Judy and I planned our funeral arrangements; I had decided to quit going to the protestant church I had been attending because I realized, the congregation did not abide by science and were getting COVID and not getting vaccinations or masking in services. They are literal Christians believing that God intervenes and protects them from being sick. I have not been back to organized religion since I left in November 2019. I also wanted to come to terms with which concept I believed in: resurrection of the body at death or re-incarnation.

Expanded horizons

In February 2022 AP is conjunct to Venus. On the encounter axis, I am playing a lot of indoor tennis. I am reading new texts on Evolutional Psychology. I have a lot of energy and am restless. Venus is on a linear connected aspect pattern opposite Uranus. I feel impatient with some people who are polarized in their thinking but don't argue with them on theory as it is a waste of time. My dream interpretations are clearer than ever before and I bring new focus to my own interpretations. I am restricting my practices to just bereavement, post-traumatic stress disorder, couple counselling and Astrological Psychology. I am doing Yoga 4 times a week to work on breathing and on relaxation. I volunteer at the Pennsylvania Prison society, joined the National Association for the Advancement of Colored People (NAACP) and am involved in a Unitarian church.

Expanded horizons yes. As you can see, I am more impulsive with organizations that represent my values than ever before in my life.

AP conjunct Venus :

Libra is on my MC and Taurus is on 5th and 6th house cusps. Both ruled by Venus. These environments are connected in my life: my relationships, my public image or main goal, and my health. As Venus takes part in assimilation and selection, I am able to compromise with people, choose friends with scrutiny and appreciate beauty in relationships and deal with relationships in psychotherapy. Chief among these Venus attributions is interest in interactions with clients, my wife, my family etc. All guided by a sense of ethical principles (Venus in Sagittarius) at best, and at worst opportunism, presumption and flightiness[54].

---

[54] Huber, Bruno & Louise, *Life Clock*, p. 186-187

5.2.5 Annie

Annie was born in France but has lived in England for many years. Her experience from LP 12 and into the 1st house seems dominated by Saturn and Pluto.

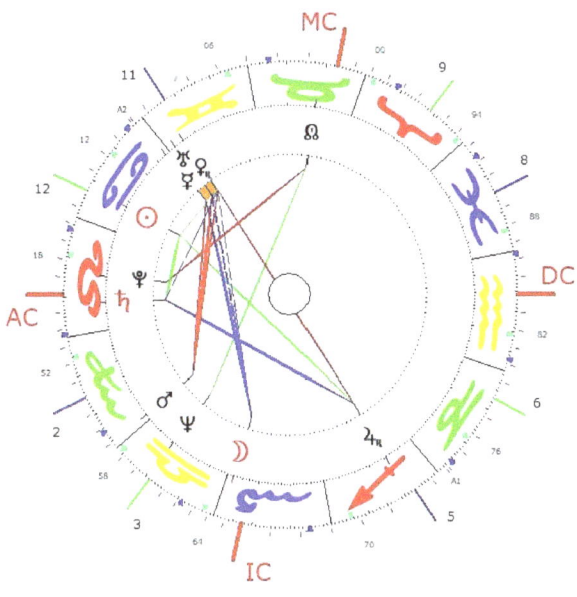

Figure 22 Annie, 14/07/1948, 0800, St Nazaire, France

2018, LP 12

LP12 was marked by the sudden and totally unexpected death of my nephew's wife Stephanie the day before her 40th birthday. She was leaving 2 young children of 11 and 8 respectively. This was a big emotional shock that brought up huge emotional memories of growing up in the shadow of death. As a child, my sense was of being an orphan even though my mother was alive but grieving and withdrawn. My ancestral family line shows death and abandonment across the generations and I felt so distressed for those two children being caught up in this family pattern that I had put so much energy into healing. It made me very aware that the process wasn't complete yet and that I shouldn't see myself as the one to decide when or how it would end.

Stephanie's death therefore served as a trigger for great sadness, emotional helplessness and hopelessness. This was compounded by the proximity of Pluto in the stress area. I entered what I would call a twilight period when I distanced myself from everyone and pretty much everything. I simply closed off and turned inwards. Each experience we live through offers us many opportunities for personal growth. Some are joyful and others are very painful.

LP 12 in Leo also corresponds to Age 70 – a new decade – and with it, the need to face our own aging and mortality. In my own strongly I-sided chart, questions of identity came up: who was I? how did I appear to people? how did I fit in the world? what was my place? A very difficult period, compounded by the saga of Brexit.

With the AP over Pluto in the stress zone, I became obsessed with thoughts of death and decay. I resented old-age and grieved for all that I had to let go of: my looks and the way I viewed myself. Images of my past came to haunt me. I cried inwardly for the self that I could have been all these years ago, for all the wrong turnings I took, the many mistakes I made but also all the opportunities that I passed by. The test of acceptance was really hard.

2020-21, crossing the AC

At the time the AP crossed the AC and came into conjunction with Saturn, the country was in lockdown which suited me as it gave me the excuse to remove myself even further from any social interactions. With Saturn at the door of my chart, I find it a challenge to openly face the world at the best of times and much prefer to remain hidden. So lockdown was very comfortable.

2022

The AP has finally moved away from Saturn and is soon to enter Virgo. I suddenly feel much lighter in mind and spirit as if the grey cloud that had been hovering overhead has finally shifted and the sun is beginning to make an appearance. I am ready to reintegrate the world and start interacting again, meeting friends for coffee, going to the cinema, attending concerts, planning holidays etc. I am able to look forward and see possibilities as well as limitations. I experience a new openness. I am now back into adult mode, well grounded and responsive and no longer the fragile little leaf that could be trampled any time. I have never fully connected to the sign Virgo before. It is my only tenanted Earth sign and I have always preferred the Air and Water temperaments. However I am coming to appreciate the lightness and flexibility of this gentle sign.

5.2.6 Lily

Lily reflects on her journey from LP 12 and into the 1st house, noting echoes with earlier life experience.

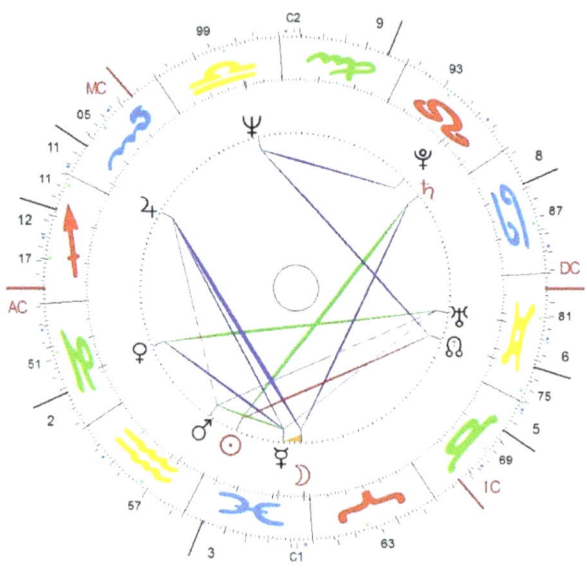

Figure 23 Lily, 23/02/1947, 0415, Whitley Bay, England

Sagittarius

During the journey of my AP, over the AC to where it is now, there have been very few notable events or changes in my personal circumstances or relationships except those relating to a number of social and political changes in the outer world. However on reflection, I am aware that significant, subtle inner changes have taken place, particularly relating to the LPs or the AP's ingress into a new sign.

In order to orientate myself I am beginning at LP 11 and the sign change from Water to Fire. After several intense years caring for my elderly parents, I was with them both at the time of death. This was a sad but profoundly emotional and spiritual experience; very life affirming and enriching. As my AP moved into the 12th house, with no further caring responsibilities, a more settled period with greater financial security (inheritance), opportunities to travel and plan various changes then followed.

LP 12

AP approaching LP 12 (around age 70): in spite of apparent good health, I experienced increasing anxiety and pessimism about the ageing process and was very dismayed about my upcoming 70th birthday. Although always being reasonably politically, socially and ecologically aware, around this time I also began to worry much more than previously about the health and future of the planet and general state of the world. The government's policy of austerity impacting many people's lives, the vote to leave the EU, Trump's election and Grenfell Tower fire etc all added to this. As many other people did at the time, I developed a heightened awareness of the role political systems play in creating inequality and suffering in the world. With Jupiter close by, for fear of being overwhelmed, I tried to resist feeling too much empathy for people who were suffering in some way. For example during news reports following the Grenfell fire. I found myself thinking "what if I could feel all those people's pain and suffering in my body, all at the same time? What would it feel like? How would I bear the pain?" With my AP moving through the Stress Zone towards the AC I then began to feel increasingly angry and militant about many social issues and could appreciate how some people give their life, fighting for a cause they really believe in.

Over the AC, echoes

AP's passage over AC (age 72): Covid emerged around this time and I experienced the resulting lockdown as a welcome opportunity to press life's 'pause button'; time and space for inner reflection. With the outer world eerily silent and none of the usual distractions, my internal world became more vivid. This time also felt like a turning point, a period of cleansing or a new beginning. I began to feel completely centred and in touch with my inner resources, creativity and power and very content. It was almost a reconnection with the sense of omnipotence I may have felt as a very young baby. At the opposite point of my chart, around the DC, I have a clear recollection of a similar period of time in my life when once recovering from a very bad dose of flu. Although not having yet come across the Hubers or the AP, I remember being very aware that this was some kind of turning point in my life, the halfway point of my 'three score years and ten'. I still have a book I bought at that time, in which I wrote 'halfway there' inside its cover. During that time I sensed that I was moving into some kind of new phase or consciousness but could not imagine how my life might unfold, let alone ever being as old as 72! Of course I now can relate this to LP 6 and APs passage over the DC.

Taurus, echoes

AP moving through 1st house (age 72 onwards): for me there was no sense of renewal of energy or the urge for new initiatives. It is difficult to know whether I might have felt differently if the pandemic had not happened but events around this time seemed to re-direct my energy from outer world to inner. Rather than having the urge to plan or initiate new activities, I became more content to appreciate and enjoy the efforts and achievements of others without any feeling of wanting to be part of anything or any feeling of envy or regret. Soon after this, the AP's passage from Fire to Earth (Capricorn) brought another unexpected and puzzling change in my attitudes and outlook in life. With a Linear/Mutable chart I had previously been fairly adaptable and stimulated by the prospect of change, both in my general attitude to life and on a day to day level. Although possibly compounded by the scarcity of some resources during the first stages of the pandemic, as my AP moved into an Earth sign, I found myself wanting to consolidate, preserve and protect e.g. keep things the same, save money and reluctant to try new things or visit new places etc. I also developed an increasing attachment to my 'old, familiar things' e.g. shoes, clothes, household items etc, becoming reluctant to discard them, even when past the point of looking respectable or even useable. If a replacement for something was suggested, it became a running joke that I would say "yes …. but I like my old one best". I can only relate this change in my attitude and behaviour to a sensitivity to Nodal AP moving through Taurus, AP approaching Venus in Capricorn / progressed Sun in Taurus perhaps. This period of conservation, reduction and retraction perhaps echoes my experience of the AP's movement the first time around my chart. Although I was a wanted, much loved first child, my parents did not have many material resources and perhaps there was a general atmosphere of austerity and scarcity after the war. Psychologically they were quite chauvinistic in their attitudes and they tended to keep themselves to themselves. My mother in particular tried to keep me safe, protecting me from any physical dangers and psychologically from what she perceived as undesirable influences outside the home. I was therefore not allowed to play with other children very often or encouraged to take risks. By nature I was quite a quiet, shy child in any case and unfortunately this family culture did not support me in learning the skills necessary to interact with other people with confidence and without self-consciousness.

It is interesting that during the same time period on the opposite side of my chart, AP from LP 6 to LP 7, (age approx 33-39) I experienced a time of social development and extroversion. With my children growing up, my horizons expanded, although still often acting unconsciously and unsure of my direction and purpose in life, I developed more friendships and took part in local classes and activities. When I look at diaries I kept around that time, I cannot believe how busy I used to be! My career also began to progress well. Working and socialising with a variety of people from all walks of life I think I was eager to learn from them, the social skills and confidence in encountering and interacting with others I had not been taught in my formative years. At the same time, while I enjoyed this phase of life and the outside world saw me socialising and performing quite successfully, with an I-sided chart and conditioning, this always took quite a lot of internal energy and came at an emotional and physical cost.

LP 1

AP currently close to LP 1 (age 75): with my AP journey from LP 12, over the AC to where it is now, I am able to view the previous years of my life, particular on the 'You' side of my chart from an objective vantage point. Almost acting as an overhead lantern, I feel 11th house Jupiter has illuminated this period of life and I have been able to develop a much deeper understanding of all that has gone before and my unconscious motivations. My parents lived well into their 90s, so I fondly imagine that I have many more years to live. However, I still have a sense of time running out and notice I am beginning to mentally prepare for the last phase of life, bringing the possible loss of my husband or our physical independence. A few of my contemporaries, friends and neighbours have become very ill or died recently and this has made me increasingly aware of the brevity and fragility of life.

In the last few weeks I have been recovering from a particularly nasty fall. Miraculously no bones were broken but I severely bruised my ribs, hip and leg on the right side of my body and sprained my left foot and had the symptoms of shock for a few days afterwards (AP not quite quincunx Uranus but close). Although I am now slowly regaining mobility and in much less pain, this was a completely unexpected, salutary experience, bringing home to me in no uncertain terms how life can be turned upside down in the blink of an eye. Having been physically 'out of action' for a while and with my AP once again at a LP, I seem to have been given the time to reevaluate things, reflecting on not only how much I depend on my physical body and the people around me, but also on my inner resources and how much I rely on these to self-regulate and help me through difficult situations. At this stage of my life, self-knowledge and a sense of wholeness and self-sufficiency continues to give me security and a sense of peace and I find that the appreciation of the cyclical nature of historical events, the rhythms of nature and a growing understanding of how my life fits with a wider universal scheme of things, reassures me greatly. I look forward to seeing what the future brings.

5.2.7 Hermann

This narrative for Hermann was written by his partner Elsbeth Houser[55]. There are strong echoes between his first and second experiences of the 1st house.

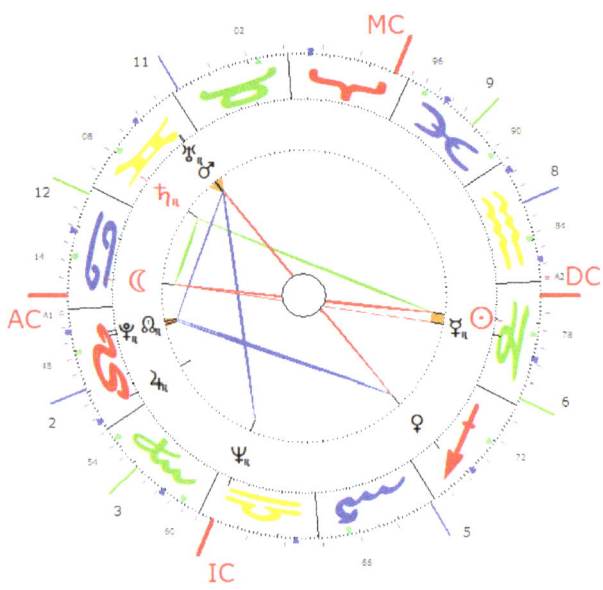

Figure 24 Hermann, 10/01/1944, 1720, Reutlingen, Germany

House 1 first time, Crossing Point, Pluto

Hermann was born in Reutlingen/Germany, during World War II. His father was in the army at that time. His mother and father were not married at the time of his birth. She was a help in the house of some rich family and gave birth to Hermann at their home. All other houses in this street were destroyed by a

---

[55] Elsbeth Houser finished basic astrological studies with Bruno Huber's last Diploma seminar www.hauser-astro.ch

bomb attack but the one where Hermann was born remained undamaged (Leo-Jupiter in 2 !?). His mother was allowed to keep Hermann with her all the time and so they developed a very strong bond.

When his father returned from WWII, he immediately occupied the position of the most important person in the household and Hermann lost his role as little prince (Crossing Point 1: March 1945). This ended in a very difficult father-son-relationship. Hermann told me that his father was psychologically and physically violent towards him and this is confirmed by his oldest sister (AP conjunction Pluto: 20th January 1947).

House 1 second time – 72-year echo

During our 21 years of private relationship and 14 years of common business activity I could see the effect of this childhood trauma in Hermann's behaviour: he has an almost compulsive need to control and dominate situations and other people and this, to the extent as if his life was in danger.

Working together in our own company until 2016 (Hermann being 72) he then retired but became more and more restless, unhappy and aggressive (Crossing Point 6th March 2017). He wanted to take over my share of our commonly owned apartment, explaining that it would be easier to handle if one of us died. At the end of the day, I agreed and the transaction was made in December 2017. In April 2018 he told me that I should look for another place to stay.

In September 2018 I bought a nice apartment some 20 km away in the high mountains (very appropriate for a Capricorn) and moved out of the place where we had shared our lives, and where I had done the lion's share of looking after the household, health care and socialising (Age Point conjunction Pluto 20th January 2019).

Very interesting to me is the fact that Hermann had to experience the first Crossing Point and AP conjunction with 1st house Pluto in a passive and suffering way that he could not consciously change or escape. To my surprise, he produced the same feelings of being left alone and abandoned (by his own active choice) during the second contact with Crossing Point and Pluto.

Meanwhile we have a very good and balanced relationship, sometimes stay alone, sometimes stay together at his or my home, spend holidays together, and help each other if needed and/or wanted.

5.2.8 Will

Will reflects on his life since his diagnosis with Chronic Fatigue Syndrome at age 69.

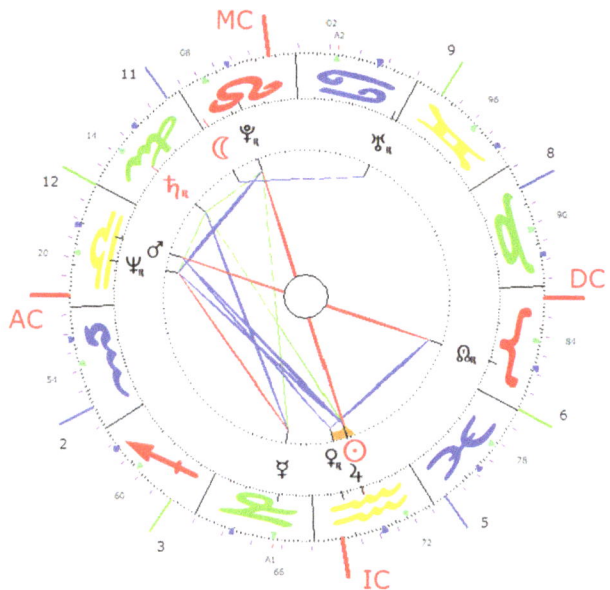

Figure 25 Will, 03/02/1950, 2350, Cheltenham, England

Will has studied Kabbalistic Astrology and understands the significance of the Saturn cycle. He says, "70 years of age is the end of 5 and a half cycles of Saturn, ie. the 5th time Saturn is in opposition to its position at birth... it matches LP 12 at age 70."

Age 69, 2019, AP approaching LP 12 – written in 2019

I have been suffering probably for a long time but since age 68, (AP conjunct Mars, opposite North Node) or before in a pretty serious way from CFS [i.e. chronic fatigue syndrome, a.k.a. M.E.] – all the classic symptoms – diagnosis over a period and recently went to the CFS/ME clinic – actually helpful, lovely lady. The 'effects' come and go, though the tiredness/aching is pretty continuous, there's quite a lot else. Some days [often without obvious trigger] I'm really low in energy [also without obvious trigger,] I might be relatively much better for a few days, then bam back to days of low… I'm okay, riding with it, learning acceptance [for its own sake but as a step towards healing too.]

The plus side, if there is one, is I'm having a lot more 'down time' just sitting, relaxing doing little which has not been my way for – well, for ever really… so it's a new learning, how to pace myself carefully… actually in many ways the worse thing is being very sensitive… I can listen to continuous loud music but if I'm sitting quietly and something suddenly makes a noise [particularly if it is sharp/clanky] I jump out of my skin!!

36 year effect – astrological comment on nodal axis on 6/12 Existence axis by author

The nodal axis in astrological psychology is significant in terms of personal/spiritual growth and awareness[56]. It's more commonly found that people will live and experience life in the house where the south node is placed, and need to develop and cultivate the opposite realm of life, where the north node is, to create a balance. In some cases, the individual will ignore one end of the axis and live almost exclusively at the other. Will's north node is strongly positioned in active Aries and is close to the BP in the 6th house, on the Existence axis. His working life

---

[56] Huber, Bruno & Louise, *Moon Node Astrology*, HopeWell 2005

as a psychotherapist has been dedicated to helping others, a strong example of living/working in a 6th house profession.

Will has offered feedback on this: in 1981, with AP conjunct the north node, he completed his training in psychosynthesis, and throughout 1982, with AP opposite Mars, in addition to working professionally as a psychotherapist he began running the Way of Qabalah courses, using distance learning but seeing individuals for training sessions. This was an intensely busy period of his life.

It's worth noting that his chart has a virtually empty "You" side[57] which leaves the central core of the chart – the self – exposed. His south node is in the 12th, conjunct Mars. When his AP was conjunct Mars and south node, his chronic fatigue syndrome demanded attention and the need for personal down time for himself, which had been ignored, emerged.

Age 71, 2021, AP conjunct Neptune in 12th and approaching AC – Will in 2021

Back in childhood I used to kick and scream at the thought of going to a party, for example, but once there I would become 'the life and soul' of the event. This has persisted all my life. Even when I was leading all those hundreds of training groups, giving talks [sometimes to very large numbers], it would be the same: hating the thought/feeling of doing it and then, once there, being very present and engaged.

I learned to frame it in the language of Carlos Castaneda. It is about 'shifting the assemblage point' – this is a very useful

---

[57] Empty you-side of the chart means that there are no aspect lines between the DC and the chart centre. This suggests a vulnerability to the outside world that is difficult for the person to defend.

description. Small shifts happen all the time but the assemblage point gets, as it were, 'stuck' in habitual positions and resists the 'pressure' to 'behave' as required to a situation. Of course, practices to loosen this stuckness abound in psychosynthesis, but knowing is one thing, doing is another.

These words are inadequate to describe something indescribable in words, that shifting of the assemblage point I just described is about moving it 'up' and 'down' as if it were on the same energy strand. I suspect it is this sort of activity I've been at for so many years, often without giving proper attention to recouping my energy after such encounters, that has brought on chronic fatigue. But the positive side of the CFS is that it has opened up a whole other level of sensitivity to both human and non-human energy fields.

Age 72, 2022, AP crossing AC in Libra and into 1st house – Will in 2022

CFS: well, the 'effects' change over time and there are periods when it recedes largely but the received wisdom [medical and alternative] is that "true" CFS does not ever completely go away, it is a truly 'chronic' condition – and lasts a lifetime. Esoterically, it is a blessing in that it is a final challenge for the soul in incarnating as a body. So I'm delighted if I hear that xxxx is doing much better – as truly I am too. But I am not looking at it in terms of 'cure' – rather as 'management'.

The essence of disidentification is that "you have it rather than it having you" – so once 'you have it' then you have a choice what to do about it – i.e. how to make it an integral part of Self rather than holding it as separate or dissonant. Indeed, I love CFS and the gifts it has given me; of course, I abhor the pain and suffering [there has been and sometimes still is both] but the more it continues the more I learn to free myself of attachments and identifications, opening the space for the "psychoenergetic" reality of existence to be manifest as my physical existence.

I have learned to manage my energy better than ever before, both in a passive sense of trying to be careful not to overdo it, but also in a more active sense of working with energy – something I've engaged with most of my adult life: lots of occult, mystical, esoteric, magical, shamanic practices etc. And CFS/ME has taught me more about my energy bodies because it constantly touches me. I know now, for me anyway, that the condition, as well as affecting my physical body, also affects my etheric, astral and causal bodies. It has loosened the 'tightness' of my assemblage as a human and I can shift so quickly now – when I choose… Sometimes of course the choice has to be not to do anything other than rest.

I remember in the Castaneda books whenever he did some intense energetic manoeuvres, he had to rest for days afterwards – reading that in my 20s I had no conception of what that meant, or the need for it. No wonder I am where I am now, but thankfully the gift of CFS/ME is this finally getting through to me. Even my consultant picked it up: she told me I needed to 'do nothing.' I said: well, I do a lot of meditation – that's not doing nothing she countered; well, I sit around a lot just reading or thinking or… – no, no, she said, that's not doing nothing… you have to learn to do nothing and that means doing nothing at all – even not doing 'doing nothing.'" A wise zen teaching indeed!

5.2.9 Peter

Peter looks at a specific example of the 36-year 'echo effect' in his life and chart.

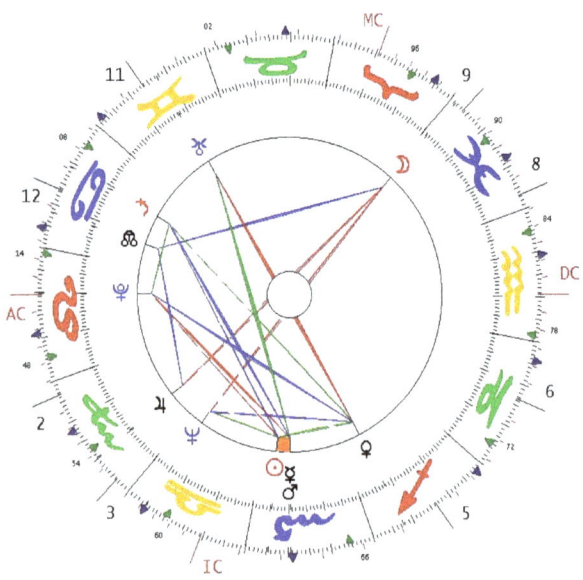

Figure 26 Peter, 28.10.1944, 2345, Lincoln, England

The period 1978-1986; LP 6 to cusp 8

This time period was a journey mostly through Aquarius, coming up to and going over the DC, opposite Pluto, and into the upper conscious part of the chart. It was a time of expansion, exploration and, yes, transformation. I was stretched by new ideas and experiences, inspirational writers such as Alan Watts, Fritz Perls and new social interactions and relationships, at the same time as learning to bring up two then-very-young children.

For this narrative I will particularly pick out one relationship which blossomed over this period – an on-off, agony-ecstasy coupling that was always causing stress in my life. And this person was not really aligned with the spiritual aspirations that were being raised in me at the time. Entry to Pisces, followed by the 8th house saw a dramatic change, as I moved work role to a more demanding job in Manchester and terminated this somewhat traumatic relationship. From hereon I was moving closer and closer to that 9th house Moon and my philosophical ideals were being stimulated.

36 years later: the period 2014-2022; LP 12 to cusp 2

In the corresponding period 36 years later, AP was passing over the AC and Pluto, mostly in Leo. Much of this time was spent in struggling to get rid of responsibilities accumulated since retirement from fulltime work around the MC. This was finalised with the closedown of the organisation I was effectively running in the first half of 2022, around the midpoint Pluto-Jupiter. Pluto had done its job. This was a new beginning.

With regard to that earlier relationship there had been no contact since 1986. I suppose there was a need within me to settle accounts in some way and become reconciled. So, in July 2021, almost exactly on LP 1, we reconnected by WhatsApp with that aim of reconciliation and the promise to be kind to each other. This lasted for a while in an amicable manner, but eventually old patterns began to surface, and the relationship again became stressful, culminating in an almighty messaging row a year later. After a long break, the final split came in

November 2021, pretty well 36 years after the original break-up.

In a way, the reconciliation was impossible at that time, as the two individuals involved were at different stages of the 'role to soul' process.

Perhaps the conflict was necessary to propel me forwards in the direction of soul, and away from earlier ego concerns.

5.3 Stories from the 2nd and 3rd Houses

We have had less input from the 2nd and 3rd houses, which is perhaps indicative of the preoccupations of people at this stage of life. There are not so many of them, and they are perhaps not so disposed, or able, to sharing their life experience and astrological insights with researchers.

5.3.1 Heinz

5.3.2 Sue

5.3.3 Maria Theresia

5.3.4 Ian

5.3.1 Heinz

Heinz reflects on his journey from age 65 to 80, and particularly the learning and moving on from experiences early in life.

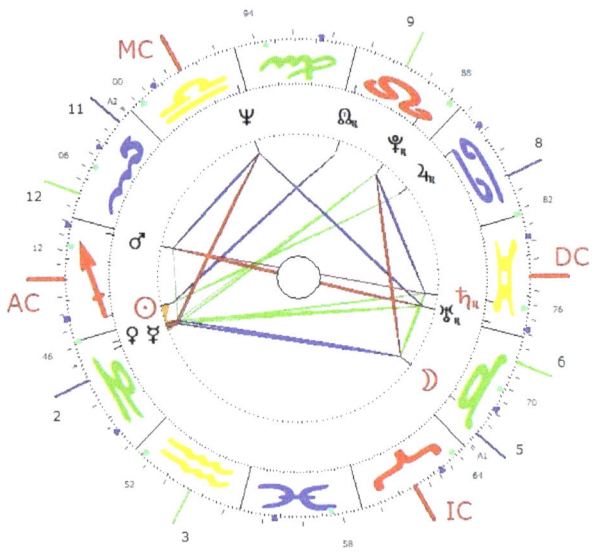

Figure 27 Heinz 18/12/1942, 0728, Würzburg, Germany

12th house and retirement

After I retired in 2008, at age 65, and my AP entered the 12th house, I scaled back my interaction with the environment and focussed on my inner development. I somehow had the feeling my life was changing in terms of developing more inner depth. I took four weeks to walk the Camino de Santiago which helped relieve my inner tension.

As my AP moved towards LP 12, I began to familiarise myself intensively the books of Alice Bailey, I didn't just read the books, I tried to become aware of what they meant in practice. I wrote two books for my granddaughters: "Recognise who you are. Be free!" and self-published them.

Through my daily meditation I have always received new impulses, one of them has been to explore events from my childhood. Thoughts about these, and the inner emotions, have occupied me very much. I have worked to forgive other people or ask them mentally for forgiveness and my past-related thoughts, bit by bit, leave me. However, with some bitter thoughts it was often, and still is, a difficult process.

When my AP was on LP 12, I held up the inner mirror to myself and realised that many events and experiences from my past were necessary to develop my personality from my own experience. Ages 66 to 72 was a period of internal recollection and orientation. As my AP travelled through the 1st house I found an abundance of thoughts and emotions from the depths of my soul washed into consciousness. I became more aware that it is not self-confidence that seems outward that is important, but the inner conviction that I exist, that I am there for something and that I am needed.

Around LP 12 I also began helping my son with his business activities and started doing a number of voluntary community activities..

In the 12th house, at first I didn't understand what life had in store for me. Walking the Camino and the various meditative ways inwards showed me the possibility of liberating myself from past emotions. I relate this to Sagittarius, the sign on the AC, the longing for inner freedom.

AP in 1st house, health problems, echo from childhood

The AP in the 1st house then gave me the connection between the collective and the individual. I realised that through inner forgiveness, personal maturity can be reached, and I feel like a mature, solid personality in my thinking, acting and speaking, able to radiate peace, serenity and goodness of heart. My current AP is in Capricorn and I continue to work on my inner goals, which I do not yet fully understand, but which return to the spiritual source.

From 2018 to 2020, from LP 1, I have had various physical health problems to do with my ears and glands – an echo of the health problems I had the first time around at age 4, when I had glandular surgery.

AP in 2nd house

Now I am in the 2nd house, I know to give thanks for everything, to forgive people, animals and nature for everything, and knowing that the bitterness I have felt has been part of my life path that has led me to where I am now. Today I am grateful for the pain and suffering that I had to experience, and am also grateful for the joy and the support that I had, even from strangers. I now recognise the meaning in everything I have experienced, all my errors and the new stage that I am now in. I understand my life better and better and I will continue to grow from it.

I look forward to the next few years with great self-confidence and optimism, with restrained peace and quiet and also with curiosity about what is to come and how I can experience it more and more consciously.

5.3.2 Sue

Sue reflects on her long process of evolution from the personal towards the transpersonal.

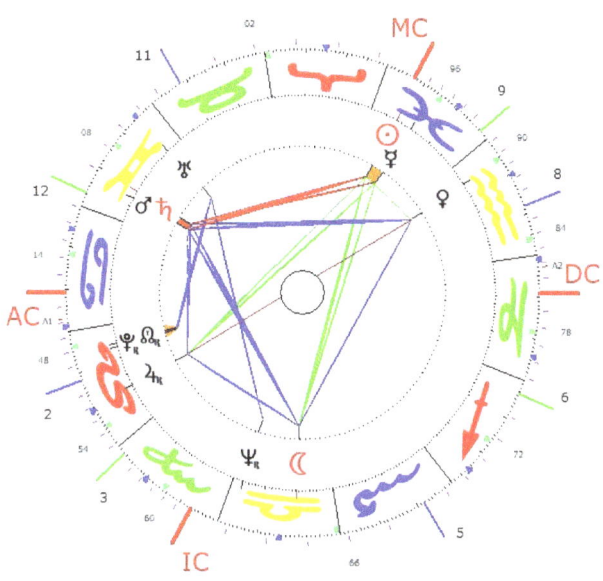

Figure 28 Sue 12/03/1944, 1328, Newton Abbot, England

Early Plutonian experiences

The quality of AP contacts the 2nd time around has been very different from my initial, Plutonian experiences – I had survived abortion attempts, been pulled into the world by forceps and it was war time; I was adopted within a month (AP trine Sun) having had virtually no contact with my birth mother.

Although my return to the 1st house has not been event-free, events have lacked the impact of those earlier AP contacts. Primarily this has been a time of reflection, of gaining more understanding of my early experiences and why they were necessary in terms of purpose and process.

The purpose

A major recurring theme in my chart is the evolution from the personal to the transpersonal. A graphic example of this is the relocation of my North Node from the personal planet structure in my Moon Node chart to the transpersonal structure in my Natal chart.

A Cancerian ascendant has the potential to evolve from a Lunar focus on selfish desires (initially necessary for survival) to a Neptunian focus on the highest expression of selfless love. The first step in this evolution is self-discovery – 'First know thyself' – and that is what I needed to work on as I made contact with the people in my world.

The process

Although the 1:7 Encounter Axis is activated at every birth, I-You issues have had continuing importance in my life through the shadow axis, nodal axis and Pluto conjunct the North Node. It would seem that all of this was needed to wean me off my South Node in the 7th house which suggests a long history of being defined by others, meeting their needs without the backing of a strong, balanced ego. To work on this, I have all 3 ego planets in a dominant learning triangle which is a component of the Representative and Model aspect figures[58] in my chart. Ego adjustment has focused primarily on an externally prominent Pisces Sun on the MC quincunx the intercepted Moon directed to focus inwards. This quincunx is

---

[58] For aspect figures Representative, Model etc, see e..g. Huber, Bruno & Louise, *Aspect Pattern Astrology*.

located on the Individuation Axis, so both arms of the Cardinal Cross are activated: time for action.

Adoption

I-You issues were intense during my early years, beginning before I knew who "I" was and when self-preservation was of paramount importance. Adoption created a lot of confusion and insecurity. My mother suffered from severe anxiety and I found it difficult to cope with this, especially as a child whose own emotional needs were not recognised (intercepted Moon in the 4th house). For a long time I saw myself as a victim and projected the blame for this onto my mother.

Neptune is also intercepted in my 4th house in Libra, so although on occasions I was quite scared of my emotionally volatile mother, I never felt alone. In the House Chart there is a one-way conjunction between Neptune and the Moon, prematurely drawing together personal needs and transpersonal love. My South Node wanted to help my mother but I didn't know how. All of this was being triggered around CP1, seeding an interest in psychology which I followed up as I approached CP2. It is quite possible that I would not have done this if I hadn't been adopted (House and Natal charts are very different). By CP3 I was developing an interest in Quantum Physics and came across a definition of light as a quantum veil behind which reality is hidden/inaccessible. Esoterically, the Moon is said to veil Neptune.

Marriage and Family

My South Node remained dominant until I was 24. With mixed motives I had entered a short, emotionally painful marriage on LP4 in intercepted Libra, which I ended as I entered the 5th house. My 2nd marriage (as AP entered

Sagittarius) was a major turning point; it gave me support and freedom and has lasted, with much happiness, for over half a century. We have a close-knit family of creative individuals and, most importantly, we are friends. We celebrate the good times and support one another when times are challenging. Most recently this happened (at LP1) and my daughter (on her LP8) bore the brunt of it. I have no clear memory of the first LP1 but was told I was a physically weak, sickly child and I do remember being sent to convalescent homes as a young child, giving me an early taste of independence which I enjoyed.

A chain of events

Developing a sense of my own identity and independence has been a long process. It began when I entered the liberating world of school (AP conjunct the North Node and Pluto). This was a massive turning point. My AP had moved from emotional Cancer to fiery Leo two years earlier and I was the other side of LP1. I was gaining in confidence, no longer feeling the need to retreat into my Cancerian shell; learning was a joy that continues to this day. As I crossed the DC, I began an Open University psychology degree: a first, truly empowering step. It gave me the self-confidence of independent decision-making and set up a chain of events:

Psychology + intellect > Huber Astrology + symbolism > esoteric studies + intuition.

I began my formal study of astrology (as AP entered 9th house) having been attracted to it for many years. Through the Hubers, I became interested in esotericism. A long-term focus has been an in-depth study of esoteric lore in relation to astrology and I have been exploring this with a small group of Huber astrologers since 2007, AP sextile Pluto. Groups have always been an important source of learning for me with both transpersonal Uranus and Saturn conjunct Mars in Gemini in the 11th house.

On the second AP conjunction to the North Node I was running an astrological workshop which included people with no astrological knowledge so I focused on an intuitive approach using the aspect structure. I learnt so much from this process, including the amount of help I was getting from the Universe in terms of content, moving to Zoom because of the pandemic, creating power points etc.

Vulcan

The sense of separateness between I and You is a powerful illusion, an attribute of Neptune as it dissolves the boundaries between the real and the unreal. My natal chart has 2 separate aspect structures: one contains all the personal planets in a large fixed structure, the other has all the transpersonal planets and the North Node in an all-blue linear structure that intersects the personal one. Planets and the North Node in the transpersonal structure span just three degrees and are therefore experienced by AP in rapid succession. Quantum physics has shown that there are two inter-related realities – the visible/material world of things and the invisible realm of potentiality. Soon after AP conjunct Pluto, as a result of working with Vulcan which exists only at the esoteric/invisible level, I became aware that there was a powerful energetic link, forged by the Cosmic Blacksmith, between the personal and transpersonal structures. Using physical planet orbs, Vulcan is conjunct the Sun in one structure and opposite Neptune in the other.

A light house

I see this as a positive milestone on my journey to integrating I and You into We – a Neptunian concept of identity, that goes way beyond sharing and is beyond my reach at this time. There is no quick fix to the transpersonal. However, there are encouraging insights from time to time. The esoteric seed thought for Cancer is "I build a lighted house and therein dwell". For over 30 years (as AP entered Pisces) I have had a log cabin in the garden for astrological work and meditation. When working in it at night, it is a physical manifestation of my "lighted house".

Going Back

Neptune is the planet of fusion and when my son was born (AP trine Pluto) I decided to trace my birth mother and succeeded with my husband's help at a time when the law did its best to prevent this. We met (AP on 6th house cusp) and became good friends until she died 5 years later (AP quincunx Saturn); I was her only child.

War brings together people who would, most probably, never have met. In 1943, the war had brought my father from Canada, where he had lived all his life, to fight in Sicily via a brief stay in England where he met my mother; she was 18 years old and didn't discover the pregnancy until my father had left England and they lost touch. It wasn't difficult to understand her dilemma and the actions she took. Information from her enabled me to trace my father in Canada but he had died when I was 8 years old. I flew to Canada and met my large extended family on the day that AP was quincunx Neptune and we remain in regular contact.

Going forward

Transpersonal energy backfires if misused. I have a number of checks and balances to counter this. At the transpersonal level Plutonian willpower has to be used with Neptunian sensitivity or I suffer the consequences on a deeply internal level. Both of these planets require a Jupiterian expansion of consciousness, initially triggered when I passed the 11+ to the local High School. Having just re-entered the second house, I am heading for an AP conjunction with my balance point Jupiter on the 2:8 Possession Axis and wait to see how that will manifest. The 2nd house is my only contact with the Earth element by house or sign. These three planets, Jupiter, Neptune and Pluto are associated with Pisces and my Piscean Sun is at the apex of a Projection Triangle which is within a Bijou aspect figure. I feel that Huber astrology has been the jewel in that figure, helping me withdraw my projections and identify the start of a transpersonal life project.

5.3.3 Maria Theresia

Maria Theresia studied and worked with Bruno and Louise Huber. She is our oldest contributor, reporting from the 3rd house.

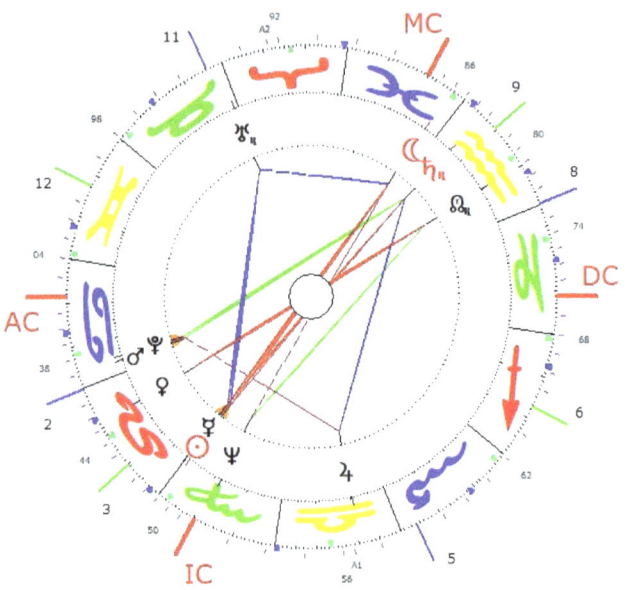

Figure 29 Maria Theresia, 25/08/1934, 0100, Uzwil, Switzerland

Background

Astrology came into my life in October 1991 – AP Trine to Venus, and just after passing over the Cosmic Rift from Pisces to Aries – into a new beginning in my life. It opened up for me like a stage curtain. I and my life stood before me, I grasped it with all my senses. Who are you really? My curiosity is great to perceive myself with my strengths and also weaknesses.

I completed all the courses, seminars of the Huber School, further training, working groups, and the API almost became my second home until Louise and Michael moved to Germany.

In 1993 I had an "aptitude interview" with Bruno for the counsellor training. I wanted to know from him whether I was suitable to become an astrological-psychological counsellor. I have this interview, like everything else from the training, on tape.

I quote the beginning of the conversation, Bruno: "First quadrant, six planets. You are predestined for people to come to you. You have made an immense experience life path with people. And you can function very well with the instrument of astrology. You have to pass on this knowledge to people. At the cosmic rift is the point where one is reborn. With you, a stillbirth, because the sign is intercepted (Aries, 10th house).

I approached this question of passing the AC for the second time with curiosity. What comes now! Now I will experience and understand what Louise meant with the casual words: "There we can then live 'That' which we could not live as a child."

LP 12 and transition into Cancer

My mother died. Mother was very formative in my life. She stood like God, life was about religion, only God, church and service counted. She had to be like that, otherwise her three children would have been taken away from her.

Ascendant sign Cancer

Seed thought "I build a lighted house to live in."

There are the people I love. Deep in me, I am an emotional person, and this shaped my life experience path very early.

The WHY question always accompanied me. In tracing the WHY, I developed like a sixth sense – to understand. The second time through, I was able to recognise and understand the connections of what I had experienced. I also became tangibly aware of the polarity in everything. My perception: the (supposedly) negative may now become a positive.

LP 1, Pluto/Mars

Pluto/Mars at the first house LP = I am the first child of my parents (I had two sisters). My father only wanted a boy. Mother told me: Father did not notice me for the first three weeks because I was not a boy. Security was a pipe dream for me − poverty, illness (my father), war and death were my childhood. Don't stand out, do everything that others want.

Pluto/Mars accompanies me through life. That's where my life experiences lie. (Quincunx to Saturn four degrees in the 11th house) − Pluto/Mars LP, Cancer sign, 1st house, big challenge. I developed a strong will to survive, and with the green energy, learning, recognising, understanding and accepting are my inner tools. When things got too much, I escaped in my mind into a fantasy world of beauty, goodness and love, this is then the other side.

LP 1 in Cancer, I was 4 years old. That was when my father became seriously ill for the first time.

LP 2 in Leo, AP conjunction Venus

Father may die. Venus at the descending lunar node!

Second transition of intercepted Leo, 2nd house (my possession). In conjunction Venus in opposition to lunar node eighth house, (die and become). 2014 saw the death of my dearly beloved husband, a month before my 80th birthday. Ten weeks later I also accompanied my sister, who was close to me, to her death. AP still conjunct Venus. Venus on the descending lunar node.

Bruno told me in the aptitude interview: The planet that is on the descending lunar node is a "gift". With "Venus" it is the ability to give harmony away, to harmonise and relax other people. It is also the feeling for colour, the feeling for beauty, that is simply all there as a quality. Also the harmony for sounds, for music, for beauty. But you also have to see the other side, that can also be degradation, a violation, not wanting to see the value of the woman in herself. Then the others come and rape you. Gift brought with "Venus", being able to feel a deep harmony. Being able to heal (Venus has to do with healing). A knowhow on the descending lunar node! Trauma can be released through the ascending lunar node.

So it is a gift that I was allowed to accompany two people dear to me into death.

The organisational aspects, decisions towards the outside, the dissolution of my sister's flat, the feeling of being abandoned and alone, I also associate with Pluto/Mars LP 1st house. Its effect is also in the 2nd house. In the second house Venus is opposite the Moon Node in the eighth house.

2nd passage of Pluto/Mars becomes a spiritual strength.

The life experiences I have had enable me to develop my own feelings, to realise my inner ideal. It is important to me that the people around me and with whom I am in contact are doing well. My feelings are like an antenna.

Bruno Huber: It is especially important to make people with Pluto in the first house understand that the effects of this planet must be beneficial and good for a larger collective. No one can grow spiritually unless it is for the good of others, as the old saying goes. This is especially true of the Pluto position in the 1st house.

Sun/Mercury third house

My first transit, Sun/Mercury 3rd house, opposite Pisces Moon and Aquarian Saturn. At age 15/16, this was the worst phase of life, for me emotionally. I couldn't fit in anywhere, felt totally at the mercy of others. A Nothing! The great fear of being exposed, of not being enough for others and of not being noticed. To be only what others want me to be.

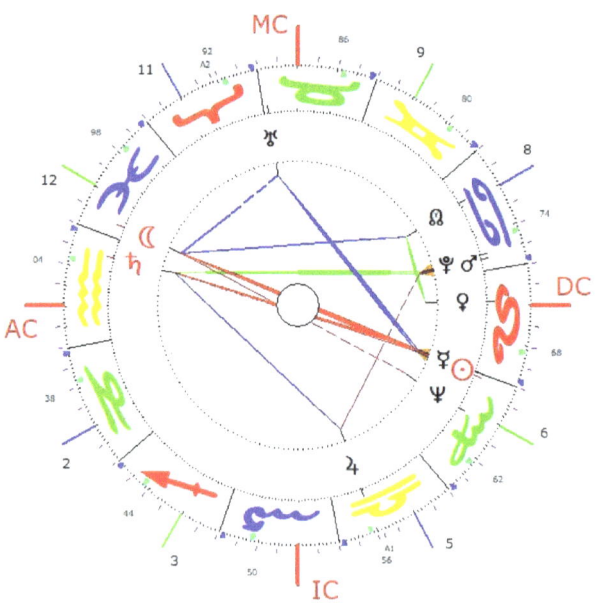

Figure 30 Maria Theresia Moon Node Chart

Looking back: My inner child was different, it would have loved to experience and share contact, exchange, joy, new things with its environment. WHY, WHY, WHY. Working with my why-questions was my development in recognising and understanding. That's when the image of my life's goal emerged in me. At that time I did not yet know that the ability to do this existed in me.

Now I am at that point again. Second time through. I am amazed at how I worked with will and consistency in my life to show that I too can learn, know, do and have. I now perceive bearing responsibility for others differently. Today I feel and realise that it is not what I do that counts, but what I am. (Transcendence of the Sun and Mercury.) The fullness of nothingness.

I wander through my Moon Node chart. My why questions turn into a big "AHA". I realise that the Moon Node chart is another layer of the personality. It is the access to the unconscious. There I can gain insight into how I would have liked to have lived. It is not unknown to me. I realise that abilities from this unconscious are present deep within me. I feel this like a "talisman" in my consciousness. From these abilities, however, further development is required in the present existence. This is where the long, often painful experiential life path has begun for me.

I perceive this reality in the present in the radix. Both themes together (radix and lunar node) have made me the personality I am today.

5.3.4 Ian

Ian is not an astrologer and has little understanding of it but is open to it and has willingly shared his experiences of life before age 70, and on into the 1st and 2nd houses to current age 80, through some traumatic family experiences.

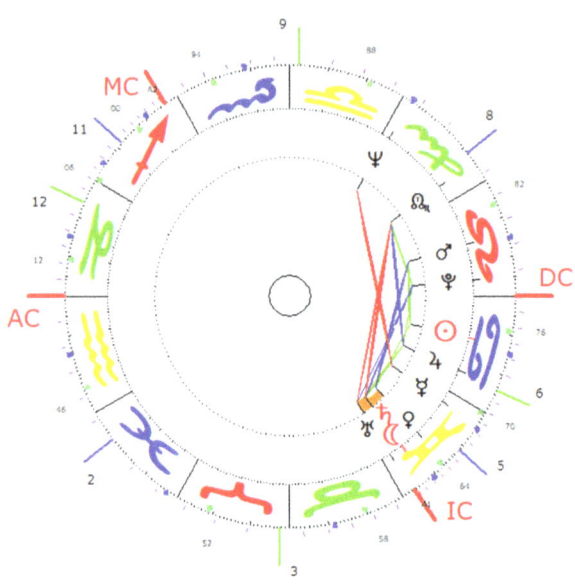

Figure 31 Ian, 09/07/1942, 2300, Lincoln, England

I fully concur with the notion of an active retirement. I often felt watching people age that you were encouraged to conform with the normative view of the aging process. Some pre-boomers and boomers are now in the fortuitous situation to challenge this model.

Retirement – Capricorn up to AC

As a grammar-school boy, I was lucky enough to end up in a generally stimulating and rewarding job and was able to retire at the age of 64 (AP enters CP) when I still had plenty of energy and hope. My first grandchild was born soon after (AP qnx UR).

Hope, given by my autonomy in the circumstances I found myself:

- Owner occupier with no mortgage
- A good pension (they are often less generous now and the retirement age rises remorselessly).
- A savings buffer built up in the good times.
- Close family living in the area.
- No particular health issues.

I was already in a caring role with a mother and younger brother who had Down's syndrome. So my social capital in terms of connections to family, friends and community was maintained.

The year after I retired, the first grandchild was born and the parents soon moved to Bedford from London. Another stroke of luck. Further grandchildren followed, when I was 69 (AP opp SO), 70 (LP12) and 72 (AP opp Pluto) all living in Bedford.

I feel changes in my approach to life have been particularly dictated by circumstance such as:

- At 69 my second grandchild died at birth (AP opp SO). This death was hugely traumatic for the family. The long-term ramifications of the death weren't remotely expected. The father wanted to move on, with the death a sad interlude, whereas the mother wanted him to be integral to her whole life experience. Eventually this divergence played out very badly 9 years later.

- At 70 my first grandchild's parents broke up. (12th house LP). Although there were difficult times, this breakup was managed fairly successfully by the parents.
- At 72 my mother died after a long period of decline (AP crosses AC and enters 1st house; opp Pluto a year later)

First house, Aquarius

I was very involved in the childcare of the three surviving grandchildren. It was often apparent that not many fathers or grandfathers were seen at play groups, nursery pickups, in outdoor playgrounds etc. I have been the only male in playgroup sessions and it is remarkable how many little kids toddled over to play.

When the kids started school it was a similar picture on the school run. A few house fathers, fathers with flexible working hours and the odd grandfather, in attendance.

- At 74 my brother with Down's syndrome died (AP opp Mars)
- At 78 the parents of my other two grandchildren broke up at the start of the pandemic (AP opp NN). There has been much traumatic family conflict since then, which I have found very difficult to handle. I have tried to support my grandchildren as much as possible, helping them through behavioural issues that have been caused by the difficult breakup. At first I tried to act as a bridge – until I was totally excluded by the father from involvement with him or his family, losing a lot of my social network.

2nd house, Pisces

- At 79 the grandchildren's last great grandparent died and the last of my mother and father's generation also died. The grandchildren's Welsh grandmother moved to Wales and nearly died in a car accident on the way.
- At 80 I was diagnosed with a serious heart problem, a traumatic experience for one who had always been healthy. (AP opp NE, moving into Aries).

Concluding thoughts

Flexibility and adaptability has been required to cope with these vicissitudes of life.

Being 'busy' with activities associated with one's own age group has never had much appeal. Activity needs to have a purpose that is often more apparent when supporting the younger generation. This has sometimes involved long term efforts to keep families in contact after marriage breakups. Children in broken families have this birthright.

Basically, whether retired or not shit happens. Even as you age you have to address and adapt to new circumstances. You realise that your influence on situations decreases (ageism in some cases?). For as long as age decline allows, you want to be available to give support to grandchildren, and children if required, but at the same time not intruding.

My outlook on life has had to adapt to 'Events, Dear Boy', on whatever scale. Since 09/11 it feels like this century is getting progressively darker both at a national and international level, with a rapid acceleration in the last two years.

Chapter 6. Conclusions

We present here some of our own conclusions following reflection on this research. The stories and charts included in this book will enable astrological researchers to make their own judgements.

The Second Time Around

Are these results in any way confirmative of the Hubers' theories about the second time around the birth chart, as outlined in Chapter 2?

Most of the responses are by those trained in Huber astrological psychology, or have been annotated by one with such experience.

We have been touched by the honesty of the respondents in revealing parts of their intimate personal story, reflecting the spirit of unflinching self-inquiry that is a characteristic of those inspired to follow the Huber Method.

It is clear that these stories show numerous correlations between their individual lives and their birth chart as interpreted in the Huber way.

There appears to be a seamless transition from 12th house into 1st house and then 2nd house, in alignment with the Hubers' theory. And in many cases the Ascendant appears to represent a major turning point in life, beginning from the 12th house Low Point at around the age of 70. Other astrological features of particular significance appear to be changes of sign, Age Point encounters with planets and Crossing Point, and its approach from the Low Point to the next house cusp (stress area).

Of course, this can never be 'proved' in a subjective approach that is not an empirical science. But we can certainly confirm that the stories are in general consistent with the theory.

The Echo Effect

The 36- or 72-year 'echo effect', whereby significant psychological events are revisited from a new perspective around 36 or 72 years later[59], is mentioned by a significant number of respondents:

>5.1.1 Kerstin
>5.1.2 Pam
>5.1.4 Sue
>5.1.8 Katharina
>5.1.9 Georgina and Paul
>5.1.11 Trish
>5.2.1 Suzanne
>5.2.2 Klaudia
>5.2.4 John
>5.2.6 Lily
>5.2.7 Hermann
>5.2.8 Will
>5.2.9 Peter
>5.3.1 Heinz
>5.3.3 Maria Theresia

---

[59] The AP makes an aspect to each planet every 6 years. The effect of this contact with the planet's energies is greatest at the conjunction and opposition aspects, i.e. every 36/72 years.

It would appear that this effect is well established for those with the eyes to see, even for those without significant astrological knowledge.

The 72-year period seems to be of particular significance, in that, as we enter the 1st house for the second time, we have the first opportunity to experience consciously energies encountered in early childhood, at a time when we had no possibility of assimilating potentially traumatic experiences.

Life Review

The consensus of the psychological 'other authors' in Chapter 3 could be summarised as follows. Life is a spiritual journey. We are born and gradually develop an ego to enable us to function in the world and have a productive life. When we get towards the stage of old age, which appears to be from around age 70 and thus aligns with 'the second time around', we become aware that life will not go on forever. And we live from thereon in the shadow of approaching death.

Our task at this stage is essentially spiritual – to prepare for that onward transition, back to whence we came. We need to reconcile with the coming transition and the psychological residue from what happened in our ego-driven years. This involves some sort of Life Review – what were the lessons, the periods of trauma in our lives, what is the residue in our bodymind[60] that we cannot take with us, can we gain the

---

[60] See eg Van der Kolk, Bessel, *The Body Keeps the Score: Brain, Mind, and Body in the Healing of Trauma*, Viking 2014 and Mate Gabor & Daniel, *The Myth of Normal: Trauma, Illness and Healing in a Toxic Culture*, Ebury Digital 2022.

insight into these events and let go, forgive ourselves and others for what happened.

If not dealt with, these things remain a drain on our psyche and our livingness. We will surely face them at the 'end', in the whole life review that is well documented as occurring in Near-Death-Experiences[61]. The theory of reincarnation suggests that we will need to go through another lifetime until we have learnt the lessons.

The Life Review process aims for a refinement of character, in James Hillman's terms[62]. We become the best person that we had the capability to become when we set out on life's journey.

The Hubers' system of Age Progression appears to provide a valuable tool to help in any process of Life Review. Of course, we can do a Life Review for ourselves at any age, simply by reflecting on the internal and external events of our lives, particularly times of major psychological change and trauma. Use of Age Progression in its full astrological depth will often provide greater and faster insight, as we become aware of the astrological factors involved at various times of our lives, and their interlinking.

Through the process of Life Review we weave the story of our lives, yet remain open to the questions: What have you still to give? What is life now asking of you?

It is suggested that, moving through this essentially spiritual process, we are preparing the ground for our own death, and

---

[61] There are now many books detailing stories of Near Death Experiences. See e.g. Fenwick, Pater & Elizabeth, *The Art of Dying*, pages 203-212.
[62] Hillman, James, *The Force of Character and the Lasting Life*.

also in the process of becoming Elders who can provide the wisdom to guide current and future generations.

Some suggestions on how to go about the process of Life Review are given in Appendix 1 on page 165.

6.4 Inner Work and Dreams

The process of Life Review involves looking at the psychological significance of different events and periods of your life. As you look back, there will be periods that you do not find comfortable, where there may be traumas or events that were not satisfactorily resolved in your psyche[63]. Your discomfort indicates that there may be inner work to be done, that is best not swept back under the carpet. The process of uncovering them, plus discussion with those close to you, may be sufficient to help you to come to terms with them.

This process may also cause some distress, as you encounter repressed aspects of your past experience. These may actually be preventing you from moving on, being trapped in patterns of the past. Ultimately, if the process is proving too difficult, you may need to find the help of a suitable counsellor (astrological or psychological), psychotherapist, psychologist or psychiatrist to help you to find a way through. It is important to seek help if it is needed.

Of course, Roberto Assagioli's psychosynthesis[64], on which astrological psychology is founded, is all about this inner work.

---

[63] See e.g. Maté, Gabor & Daniel, *The Myth of Normal*.
[64] Assagioli, Roberto, *Transpersonal Development*.

There are also numerous other approaches, notably as described in Alain Forget's *How to Get Out of this World Alive*[65].

The input from John Grove (page 108) reminds us that analysis of our dreams can provide valuable evidence to help in our psychological development after age 70, just as much as at earlier stages of life. The dream and its picturing can help illuminate particular questions and issues that we currently face.

The recall and gathering of dreams requires a level of consistent application and perseverance that does not come easily to many of us, but it is useful to be aware of this valuable tool in our armoury, particularly when a specific dream comes to the foreground of our thinking[66].

John particularly recommends Robert Johnson's book *Inner Work*[67] on how to approach the inner work that may be necessary to understand our psychological depths, and the role that dream analysis may play in this process.

Final Thoughts

Writing this book has been an instructive process for both of us, and we have been privileged to read the insights of others along their journey through the Second Time Around the birth chart, and to make them available for others to read.

It is clear that Bruno & Louise Huber's astrological psychology and in particular Age Progression and Life Review

---

[65] Alain Forget, *How to Get Out of this World Alive: The Ultimate Self-Empowerment Handbook*
[66] See section 5.2.4 John and John Grove's books *Life Passages*, HopeWell, 2017, *Dreams and Astrological Psychology*, HopeWell, 2014
[67] Johnson, Robert A, *Inner Work*.

provide a useful aid to many of our respondents in understanding their life journey. This can help identify and remove the obstacles that prevent us from progressing to the new beginnings that are possible the second time around the birth chart from age 70. If we take on board and deal with the lessons that emerge we can progress towards the realisation and wisdom that has always been our potential. And the world so needs that wisdom today.

Appendix 1. Write your own Life Review

Whether you are a practitioner using the Huber Method of astrological psychology, a student studying this approach to astrology or an interested non-astrologer wanting to know more about this method, writing your own life review is something you can do at any time and at any stage of your life.

Students of astrological psychology do a life review as part of their studies when learning to use Age Progression[68]. The exercise accompanying this topic encourages students to study the movement of the Age Point in their own chart, identifying individual events or periods of time in their lives which coincide with the Age Point making significant aspects to planets, moving into a new house, a new sign or passing over a Low Point.

Using the natal chart in this way, as a Life Clock, can help to identify significant psychological growth points in life – those from the past as well as those present and in the future. Whilst these may be positive or negative, each is a potential step on the path of individuation.

Interested non-astrologers can use the Age Point chart wheel (Figure 32 [69]), in the same way – minus the astrology – as a starting point.

---

[68] *Astrological Psychology – The Huber Method.* Chapter 6. The Element of Time: Age Progression in the Horoscope pp. 193-205. Pub. Hopewell 2017
[69] Huber, Bruno & Louise, *Life Clock*, pages 46-47.

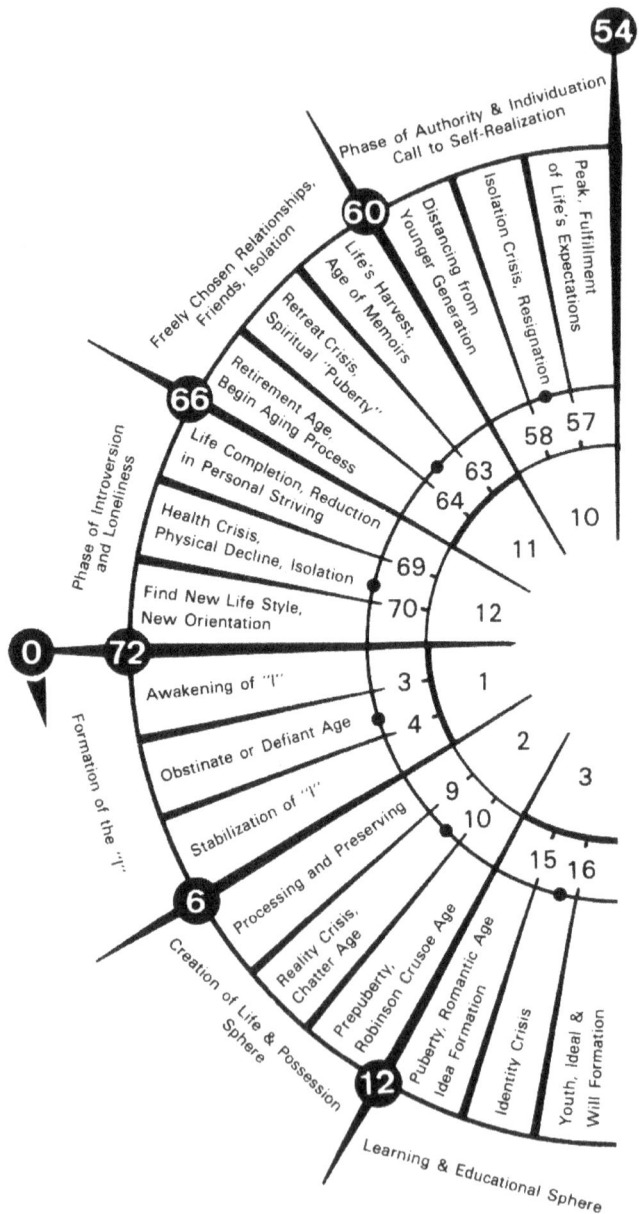

Figure 32 Keywords for the 36 life phases, from Life Clock

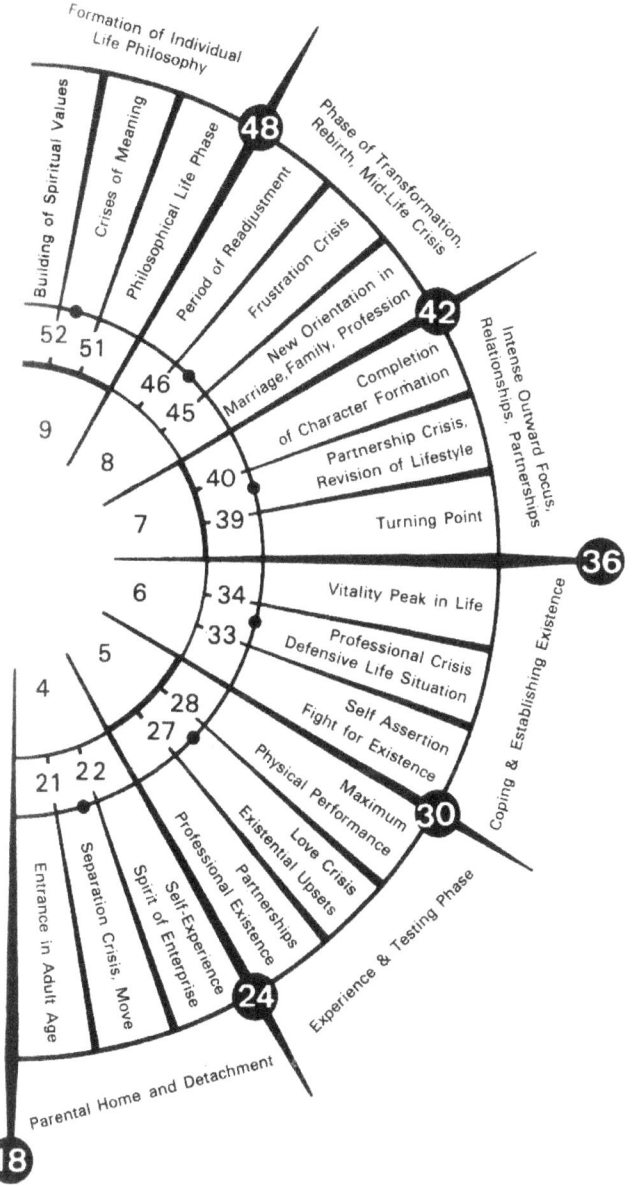

Figure 32 shows keywords for the thirty-six life phases as they are expressed through the houses of the horoscope. The suggested experiences and the life phase ages associated with them are a useful guide to help you embark on your life review. You may want to organise how you go about this, perhaps diagrammatically or with headings and/or separate pages for the different life phases.

Using Age Progression and viewing the natal chart as a Life Clock, astrological psychology enables the individual to pinpoint where they are by age, and focus on the house/area of life experience and expression where they are at any given point of the 72 year cycle, and beyond, as the Age Point makes its second circuit of the chart.

My own experience of using Age Progression and Life Clock came into its own when I was making regular appearances on a local radio phone-in programme, taking calls from listeners who asked questions about astrology and how it might help them in their lives. I talked about astrology and psychology in general terms, but one instance of the value and application of Age Progression stands out in my mind.

A man rang in asking if I could help him. He was desperate for some insights as he was going through a bad patch on a personal level as well as at work. He wanted to know if it would ever end, and what could he do. I asked him his age; he was in his mid-forties, with his Age Point in the 8th house. Between the ages of 42 and 48, many people experience some kind of mid-life crisis. Often they are frustrated and looking for a new orientation in life but may have no idea of what this might be.

The Hubers note the passage of the Age Point in the 8th house[70] as a phase of change, transformation and rebirth. What was going on for the caller reflected this phase of uncertainty and turmoil. Without the specific details of his chart to refer to, I was able to explain that what he was experiencing was pretty much spot on for this stage of life. With greater awareness that his current situation was a phase, experienced by many, and one that he could potentially grow from, and through, he was reassured and relieved.

Some suggestions to get you started

The list below is a starting point, and if the suggestions don't resonate for you it doesn't matter. The task is to get started and just focus on the progressive journey through the life phases on the chart and fill this with your own experiences. You can move backwards and forwards through time – there's no "right" way of doing this exercise. Just note ages, dates and anything relevant to each phase. For instance, you may recall a childhood memory when thinking about what was happening in your thirties and make a note of it under the "early years" heading. Memories pop up into consciousness in a random way!

If you're doing this astrologically using Age Progression, take note of the planet, house, sign involved, along with any other significant astrological features.

- Go back to your earliest memory as a baby or young child

---

[70] Huber, Bruno & Louise, *Life Clock – The Huber Method of Timing in the Horoscope* pp235 – 238, HopeWell 2006

- Reconnect with what family life was like for you as a child
- What did you do pre-school? Play alone, or with parents/ siblings? At home, in the garden or outside?
- As you grew up, what friends did you have? What activities did you enjoy (or not enjoy)?
- Did you go on holiday or travel? Which places do you remember and why?
- How did you experience school? Was it a good experience or not? Consider early years education and later teenage years.
- Did you have a part-time job while you were still at school? What did you learn about life from this?
- Did you develop your career/working life with additional study and further education?
- Did you leave home, move away, form new relationships?
- As an adult did you have a family, progress your career, take on more responsibilities?
- How did your outlook on life change, perhaps at age 36 or maybe later in your mid-40s?
- Who were, or are, the influential people on your life? At what stage of your life did they have this effect on you?
- What significant experiences of any kind, have you had, which have stayed with you and changed your attitude and outlook on life?

Prompts which might help you

Photographs, albums, personal memorabilia, music (memories can be evoked by music and songs), books and stories you loved as a child, old TV programmes, diaries, personal journals and notes.

A cautionary note

See 6.4 Inner Work and Dreams on page 161.

Go to it!

The process of undertaking a life review can be a very rewarding, ongoing, exercise. It may help make you into a new person for the rest of your life; it may even evolve into a memoir!

Good luck – and enjoy the process.

Appendix 2. Survey guidelines as sent out.

Detailed guidelines for astrologers

Respondents were given guidelines and suggestions on what to consider in their feedback. Their experiences are what we were looking for, not "what the book says", in the spirit of Bruno Huber's research into the experiences of real people.

1) Suggested general observations to share:

- What have been the most significant events or happenings in life for you since LP12/crossing the AC/moving into the 1st house and beyond?
- Any personal changes in outlook, activities, interests, attitudes, values?
- Have you become a volunteer or started a new job?
- Have you made any changes in your life or come to fresh understandings, maybe about yourself in relation to others or your wider environment?
- Have you enjoyed a "second childhood" interacting with grandchildren or other younger people in your life?
- Are you seeing yourself more clearly, or in a different light?

2) Suggested Astrological considerations:

- Age 70 – LP12 – any planets in 12th house?
- Is the crossing point on the 6/12 axis? How was this for you? Was it significant?
- Experiences of the stress zone before the AC at age 72

- Age 72 – planets on or near the AC and aspects they make to other planets, especially in 7th house, on/near the DC. Conjunction & quincunx to these may be most relevant.
- Sign on the AC – has this become of greater significance, e.g. meaning of the Sign's esoteric seed thought having more relevance/depth?
- Sign your current AP is in – significance of this as background effect?
- Has your AP changed Signs during this period? How did you experience this?
- Is the crossing point on one of the axes your AP has moved through or into? If so, how was this experienced?
- Anything noted for AP going over BP 1 and LP 1, or in the CFM zones of the house?
- The 1st house is on the Encounter axis – how is or was your experience of encountering your self this time (as well as others) with life's experiences to draw upon? Are you looking at yourself anew?
- Have there been drawbacks, e.g because of health problems, and how have you coped with them?
- Have your horizons expanded in any way, or narrowed?
- If your AP is in the 2nd house all the above considerations could apply, but with an emphasis on your feelings and attitudes towards possessions, what you value, and what you fear.

- If your AP has gone over the AC it will be in the 1st Quadrant. Are you aware of a change of Quadrant emphasis – maybe of being more impulsive, but also of drawing on your intuition more consciously this time around, with all your life experience to support this?

These guidelines were intended to get the respondent started in their thought process. They were simply asked to be honest in what they shared, and only share what they felt comfortable with.

Guidelines for non-astrologers

A simplified set of guidelines were given to non-astrologers:

- What have been the most significant events or happenings in life for you since age 70 and age 72?
- Any personal changes in outlook, activities, interests, attitudes, values?
- Have you made any changes in your life or come to fresh understandings, maybe about yourself in relation to others or your wider environment?
- Are you seeing yourself more clearly, or in a different light?
- What takes priority now, and has this changed? And how?
- Have there been & are there are any new or current awakenings, changes of views, priorities and orientations on life etc?
- Any important insights?
- Has your outlook on life changed or is it changing?

- Any significant dates or years when things changed would be useful to know as well.

Further input request – the echo effect

Given the frequency of 36- and 72-year echoes, in December 2022 we issued a blog post[71] requesting further input on this particular facet of the results, from both astrologers and non-astrologers, as follows. The limited response to this request has been included for consideration in the stories in Chapter 5.

36-year echoes

As we progress through life, there are 6-yearly psychological echoes of the energies of earlier periods of life, when astrological 'aspects' are made to specific astrological features, such as planets. This effect is particularly strong after 36 years (opposition), when we re-encounter the energetic pattern of 36 years before, but from a wider or closer perspective.

If the earlier period was of great psychological significance, for example involving traumatic events or psychological growth, then we can expect some echo of these concerns after 36 years – particularly if the events were not at the time psychologically resolved. Perhaps, in some way, we reconnect with the events or the people that were involved in them, and some new insights or development can occur.

---

[71] https://astrologicalpsychology.org/the-six-and-thirty-six-years-in-huber-age-progression/

72-year echoes – the second time around

So what happens after 72 years, when we have travelled through these 12 psychological life stages, the houses? According to Huber Astrology, we begin again at the point of birth (Ascendant=AC), and travel through the 12 houses again. From here on, we encounter energy patterns that we first experienced in childhood, then adolescence, then adulthood.

This is like the 36-year effect above, but now we directly encounter the same patterns again. So, an unresolved trauma at, say the age of 3, may suddenly become a significant psychological issue at age 75, if it was not resolved around age 39.

Note that both the 36-year and 72-year echoes, while a consequence of Huber Astrology, do not require any significant astrological knowledge or generation of a birth chart to be understood.

When it comes to considering the 36-year effect (or the 72-year effect), a person who is aware of their internal psychological process through life may become aware of this effect, without any knowledge of astrology. Quite remarkably, we have an effect predicted by Huber Astrology that does not require any astrological knowledge to understand.

Bibliography

Assagioli, Roberto, *Transpersonal Development: The Dimension Beyond Psychosynthesis*, Inner Way, 2008

Bailey, Alice A.,
  A Treatise on White Magic, Lucis Press, 1934
  Esoteric Healing, Lucis Press

Fenwick, Peter and Elizabeth, *The Art of Dying*, Bloomsbury 2008

Forget, Alain, *How to Get Out of This World Alive: The Ultimate Self-Empowerment Handbook*, Lulu, 2012.

Greene, Liz,
  Relating – An Astrological Guide to Living with Others on a Small Planet, Coventure, 1977
  Saturn: A New Look at an Old Devil, Weiser, 1976.

Grove, John,
  Life Passages, HopeWell, 2017.
  Dreams and Astrological Psychology, HopeWell, 2014

Hillman, James,
  The Force of Character and the Lasting Life, Ballantine, 1999
  The Soul's Code, Bantam, 1997

Hopewell, Barry & Joyce,
  Piercing the Eggshell: The Hubers and their Astrological Psychology, HopeWell, 2020
  Astrological Psychology: The Huber Method, HopeWell 2017

Hopewell, Joyce & Llewellyn, Richard, *The Cosmic Egg Timer: Introducing Astrological Psychology*, HopeWell 2004, 2011, 2018.

Hopewell, Joyce, *Using Age Progression: Understanding Life's Journey*, HopeWell 2013

Huber, Bruno, *Astrological Psychosynthesis*, HopeWell 2006

Huber, Bruno & Louise,
  Aspect Pattern Astrology, HopeWell 2005, 2019
  Life Clock, Hopewell, 2006, 2022
  Moon Node Astrology, HopeWell, 2005
  The Astrological Houses, HopeWell 2011

Huber, Louise, *Reflections and Meditations on the Signs of the Zodiac*, American Federation of Astrologers Inc., 1984

Johnson, Robert. A, *Inner Work: Using Dreams & Active Imagination for Personal Growth*, Harper 1991

Kübler-Ross, Elisabeth, *On Death & Dying,* Simon & Schuster/Touchstone, 1969

Levine, Peter, *Waking the Tiger: Healing Trauma*, North Atlantic Books, 1997

Maté, Gabor & Daniel, *The Myth of Normal: Trauma, Illness & Healing in a Toxic Culture*, Penguin 2022

Parfitt, Will,
  Psychosynthesis: The Elements and Beyond, PS Avalon 2003/2015
  The Magic Of Psychosynthesis, PS Books 2019
  The Something and Nothing of Death, PS Avalon, 2008

Rankin, Lissa, *Sacred Medicine: A Doctor's Quest to Unravel the Mysteries of Healing*, Boulder 2022

Robinson, John C, *The Three Secrets of Aging: A Radical Guide*, O-Books, 2012

Rudhyar, Dane, *An Astrological Triptych – The Illumined Road*, Aurora Press,1978

Sasportas, Howard, *The Twelve Houses*, Aquarian Press, 1985 van der Kolk, Bessel, *The Body Keeps the Score: Brain, Mind, and Body in the Healing of Trauma*, Viking 2014

Weiner, Errol, *Transpersonal Astrology – Finding the Soul's Purpose*, Element, 1991

Zweig, Connie, *The Inner Work of Age – Shifting from Role to Soul*, Park Street Press, 2021

www.ingramcontent.com/pod-product-compliance
Lightning Source LLC
Chambersburg PA
CBHW060818190426
43197CB00038B/2077